Prayers for new Brides

Putting on God's Armor After the Wedding Dress

∽ Jennifer O. White ∾

What others are saying . . .

God's vision for your marriage is for your love story to be deeply rooted in Him in order to stay deeply in love with your husband. *Prayers for New Brides: Putting on God's Armor After the Wedding Dress* by Jennifer White gives you seeds to begin growing those roots and a love that will last till "death do us part."
> Justin and Trisha Davis, RefineUs Marriage Ministry, refineus.org

We usually relate warfare imagery to men, but Jennifer White has done an outstanding job of grabbing the attention of women and calling them to be equipped for the spiritual war taking place over marriage.
> Brandon Cox, Pastor of Grace Hills Church and editor of Pastors.com

Jennifer White does a remarkable job helping every new bride adorn herself with the spiritual armor necessary to experience a lifelong marriage of joy and influence. This is a must-have gift for every new bride.
> Joshua and Christi Straub, co-founders The Connextion Group

Marriage doesn't get better with age, we get better. Marriage makes us better. This book reminds every bride of that process but gives hope that it can begin at "I do."
> David Uth, First Baptist Orlando

Prayers for New Brides is a must-read for any bride hoping to make her marriage the sacred romance she desires.
> Angela Bisignano, PhD, www.drangelabisignano.com/blog

Following these principles will save wives time and heartache as they allow God's transforming power to work in their hearts and marriages.
> Robert and Rebecca LeCompte
> churchglorious.com, pastors of City of Faith San Diego

In *Prayers for New Brides: Putting on God's Armor After the Wedding Dress,* Jennifer White offers every new bride an extensive primer on honoring marriage as the reflection of God's perfect and enduring covenant with His Church.
> Ted Cunningham, Pastor at Woodland Hills Family Church, Branson, MO, and author of *Fun Loving You*

In this book, Jennifer White offers practical and practice-able advice. Scripture-rich and full of down-to-earth insight, this will be an asset to any couple embarking on the adventure of marriage, or to those who want to start anew in the marriage they're in.
> Jennifer Kennedy Dean, Executive Director, The Praying Life Foundation, Author of *Live a Praying Life* and numerous books and Bible studies

Writing deeply from God's Word and her own experiences in marriage, Jennifer will inspire you to passionately love God and love your husband on this life-transforming journey. You will learn to see your husband as God sees him and to pray for him in ways that will supercharge your marriage.

> Lyn Smith, LynSmith.org, Bible activist and speaker. Author of *WORD — Psalm 119: A Study in 22 Meditations* and co-author of *Think 4:8*

In *Prayers for New Brides*, Jennifer White reveals through her own story as well as Scripture how important it is for couples to know how to weather the storms, stand firm in faith, and fight for the most important earthly relationship they will ever experience. *Prayers for New Brides* will be my "go- to" gift for all newly married couples!

> Dr. Michelle L. Bengtson
> Inspirational speaker, author, neuropsychologist

This book is grounded in the Gospel, makes much of Jesus, and will help women understand their God-given role in God's economy. New brides are going to be blessed and challenged by her teaching and honesty.

> Dave Jenkins, Executive Director, Servants of Grace Ministries; Executive Editor, Theology for Life

In *Prayers for New Brides*, Jennifer White has captured the essence of where our help comes from. Praying the Scriptures not only brings help and healing but also helps us keep our focus on God and what He wants to do in our lives.

> R.G. & Karen Yallaly, Directors of Marriage Ministry, Woodland Hills Family Church, Branson, MO

In *Prayers for New Brides*, Jennifer White helps guide new brides with a real and practical way to respect and honor their husbands with prayer from the start. A bride that knows how to pray for her husband will be a blessing to any marriage.

> Steve & Pam Chapman, Executive Directors, Marriage Encounter Support Foundation, Supporting United Marriage Encounter Weekends around the world

Prayers for New Brides is a book that inspires and equips new brides in their prayer life. This is one resource I will continually recommend to the many women I serve.

> Cherie Zack, Speaker and Wife Coach, District Director of Women's Ministries, S. Carolina District Council of the Assemblies of God, Founder of The Imperfect Wives, and Co-Author of 16-Day Love Challenge

First printing: February 2015

ISBN: 978-0-89221-733-5
Library of Congress Number: 2014920452

Cover by Diana Bogardus

Please consider requesting that a copy of this volume be purchased by your local library system.

Printed in the United States of America

Please visit our website for other great titles:
www.newleafpress.net

For information regarding author interviews,
please contact the publicity department at (870) 438-5288

New Leaf Press
A Division of New Leaf Publishing Group
www.newleafpress.net

Dedications

This book became a reality out of my desire to bless Katherine White Webb and Chelse Dilmore White as they said "I do" to their sacred marriages.

It is my "God is Able" banner flying over the marriages and future marriages of Deanna White, Shanti Odom, Mary Branch, Lindsey Morrow, Shelbie Moriarty, Lydia Branch, Kaleigh Grace Morrow, Kenlie Morrow, Maria Gowan, and Sundi Jo Graham.

Acknowledgments

To my darling, David White, your faithfulness is more to me than I can express. Thank you for supporting my desire to share God's amazing power in our marriage within this book.

To Rebecca LeCompte and Cherie Zack, your prayers and wisdom molded so much of this book. Thank you for the great subtitle and so much more.

To Louanne Dietrich, thank you for building more than a house with me. Your encouragement has been nutrition for my soul!

To Mom, Big Daddy, Travis, Shanti, Nana, Dawn, Melissa, and Tami, thank you for loving me just as I am.

To the Glory Writers (my writing accountability team), you made this book better with edits and prayer.

To Tim Dudley, thank you for wanting to share this story.

Nothing is impossible with God! He is faithful. With His mighty power at work in each of us, He is able to do infinitely more than we can ask or dare to dream. My life, my marriage, and this book are evidences of this truth!

Table of Contents

A Note to the Reader

Dear Bride,

I am not writing this book because I have life with God and marriage all figured out. I am writing to you because as a wife, I have learned how much I need God.

Forty brief chapters await you. Each chapter is packed with teaching, life experiences, prayer prompts, and Scripture references. Hang on to it and refer to it as your marriage enters new stages and challenges.

If you love to conquer a book, then start at the beginning and read straight through. Then go back to the beginning and tackle the "A Wife's Call to Action" assignments at your own pace. If you savor Bible studies like a five-course meal, then divide these 40 chapters into 8 weeks. Five chapters a week will give you plenty of time to digest the concepts, dig into the Scriptures and journal your thoughts.

I've read just a few chapters of a book and experienced real life transformation. If you are just unsure about tackling this whole book, scan the table of contents for a chapter that speaks to your situation. Start there. Don't get wrapped up in doing it "right." God can use one phrase to minister to your heart.

As you read, you may find yourself wondering, "What about my husband and his responsibility?" He has plenty. But this book is focused on you and yours.

It is never too late to arm your marriage with prayer. While this book is written to a new bride, I believe every bride will find it helpful. As I reread the words of this book, I find God is reminding me and encouraging me.

My words to you assume you and your husband have a relationship with Jesus Christ. If that is not the case, I invite you to keep reading.

God is patient, gentle, and kind. He is a gentleman who never forces Himself into anyone's life. His hand is extended to you and your husband through His Word. Let this book, which is filled with His Word, give you a fresh glimpse of who He is and what He can do in your hearts and in your life together.

Your friend,
Jennifer O. White

Part 1

A Call to Battle

Introduction

You didn't dog-ear a page in the bride magazine featuring a warrior bride holding a shield in one hand with a sword in the other, did you? Admit it, the only armor you considered buying for your big day contained spandex, padding, and underwire.

Why would you need to wear armor now?

The fight to become someone's bride is finally over. It's all romantic date nights and magnificent dreams come true from here on out — right? And what is so attractive about wearing armor "over" the wedding dress? Nobody you know is pinning that picture on Pinterest!

Maybe you do have marriage all figured out. You've counted the cost of serving one man for the rest of your life and said, "I'm a great giver. I will always want to put him first and submit to him in the scariest of days. That helpmate thing . . . I've got that. On his worst day, he will be the one I will want to stand next to." You know there will be tough times, but they could NEVER compare to how much you want to be with him every single day! And he loves you unconditionally . . . right?

I don't want to bust your happily-ever-after bubble. But, here's the truth. Your earthly marriage will NEVER be perfect. There will always be two imperfect humans in your holy union. Say it with me, "I am not perfect and I do not have what it takes to be a perfect wife." And this guy you married — guaranteed to miss the mark as well. You said "I do" as two sinful (sin-filled) individuals who are on a quest to work out the oneness of marriage. As hard as you both try to love each other completely, you will struggle a bit. Why? Because until death parts the two of you, the battle between good and evil will follow your relationship. There is a war, and you, my friend, are in it.

The Bible promises that God's goodness and mercy will follow you all the days of your life (Psalm 23:6). You are never without the benefit of God's wild pursuit to guard, guide, and protect you. He is an experienced, victorious warrior and He is fighting for you.

He warns us that Satan is prowling the earth looking for opportunities to kill, steal, and destroy (John 10:10). Don't kid yourself. Satan is very aware of you and your marriage. Marriage is one of his favorite targets. The divorce rate is evidence of that. Take two minutes and count the divorces in your family, your neighborhood, and in your church community. Those couples all said "I DO" with intentions to live happily ever after — just like you.

You have to fight to stay married. And I don't mean fight each other. You are suiting up to fight your own selfish thoughts, expectations, and every social norm that does not honor God and His ways. Discouragement will certainly be knocking at your door. The temptation to give up when things are really hard will knock, and well-meaning people will be there to help you open that door.

This fight is God's fight. He is able to successfully defend you, your husband, and your marriage. But he won't force you to let Him lead the way. It's your choice to surrender to God's authority in your marriage.

Thick, invisible walls in my heart kept me from embracing a life and marriage surrendered to God. Layers of fear, doubt, and self-protection kept me running my own life and taking advice from people who had not experienced God's love and protective nature. All the while, He was standing there waiting for me to see Him loving me, ready to help me, if I would only ask.

My first marriage ended. I pulled the plug because I had not seen God. I had heard about Him my entire life. I talked about Him, taught lessons in Sunday school, lead the Fellowship of Christian Students, and joyfully served Him as a preacher's wife. But I had not experienced the reality of Him. I did not know God could save my sacred union to Michael. I did not know Jesus as the Savior of marriages.

Within a few years of my second marriage, I found myself crying out to God with a 911 plea for help. And God came to my rescue. Through Bible study and prayer, He revealed Himself to me, nurtured my wounded heart, and helped me to see more of my life from His point of view. Over time, He has convinced me of His faithful love and given me the desire to stay under His leadership. The "help me, Jesus" cries of my heart resulted in extraordinary miracles in my life and greatly affected my now-thriving marriage to David.

I'm a bit of a mother hen. I want to protect you. I want you to be prepared for the war against your marriage. I want you to begin your marriage knowing that God is your "go-to" guru for enjoying your long life together. I want you to see how marriage relates to the gospel of Jesus. I want to encourage you to let Jesus be your model for loving your husband.

This book is what I would share with you if we could sit together for a few hours and talk about marriage. I've packed it with how I've learned to let God lead me as David's wife. There are prayer prompts to guide you in surrendering your way for His ways. And I'm giving you tactical missions, A Wife's Call to Action, to help you fortify and act on your faith in God.

Your marriage journey can be a light to the world, a city on a hill where people see God. I would love to hear from you and learn from your experiences too. Join me at prayersfornewbrides.com.

But the Lord is faithful. He will establish you and guard you against the evil one (2 Thessalonians 3:3).

Marriage: A Battle Worth Fighting

Marriage is so much like salvation and our relationship with Christ that Paul says you can't understand marriage without looking at the gospel.[1]

> — Timothy Keller, *The Meaning of Marriage: Facing the Complexities of Commitment with the Wisdom of God*

Chapter 1

The Significance of Your Marriage

The act of marriage is God's idea. He planned this beautiful union between Adam and Eve and brought it to life. God, your Creator, did not waiver as He spoke life into their bodies and into their holy "ever after" relationship. His Word paints the true picture of marriage and shows us how significant married love truly is.

God designed marriage to reveal His relationship to the Church. With deep and lasting love, God has promised to remain faithful to His people (you and me). His kindness and mercy for His Bride is constantly renewed despite the many faults of every Christ follower. Can you see, in His unconditional love, a neon sign pointing to a marriage that endures for better or worse?

Like the gospel of Jesus Christ, the relationship between husband and wife is simple and yet enormously important. Your sacred union should reflect the faithful, serving love of Jesus toward His Church. The Body of Christ represents the unity created between Jesus and the redeemed. Jesus' giving, others first, and love "no matter what" attitude is required to fulfill the covenant between man and wife.

Being married is beautiful. The idea of two people becoming one is full of mystery and intrigue. It involves more than this book could begin to describe. And you get to explore it from now until forever.

You've stepped into a drama, a comedy, and a thriller that will transform you and your beloved into one entity. Life together is unpredictable. It will offer you plenty of suspense. There will be beautiful scenes, romantic moments, pandemonium, and edge-of-your-seat situations. All of these are best viewed through the lens of God's manual for living and loving. Otherwise, they will cause a drift that will lead to worshiping someone or something other than God.

Adam and Eve found themselves worshiping their own desires, and the consequences were huge! You've been exposed to people who do not fully embrace God's plan for marriage. In the media and in your community, you've witnessed the attack on marriage. Imperfect people sometimes choose to solve problems with adultery, abuse, addictions, pornography, same-sex relationships, and divorce. Our self-obsessed culture struggles to choose the selfless ways of God's Son.

The evil influence has been subtle, consistent, and pervasive. The end game is to have you desire the opposite of what God calls beautiful. How will you and your husband hold fast to God's plan for a beautiful and lasting marriage? Do you believe it's possible to remain faithfully married and enjoy life together as God intended? Today, I believe it wholeheartedly. But I have fought hard to believe God over the other influences in my life. I've passionately and desperately pursued God's will over my own by praying His Word back to Him.

My heart's desire is for you to proactively wrestle your will to the ground and allow God's will to be the strength of your marriage. Knowing Him and embracing His plan are the epic ingredients to accomplishing this necessary duty. It took me several years into my second marriage and a significant crisis to become someone who yields to God instead of being the captain of my own ship. Today, I am celebrating that you have the opportunity to be far more prepared.

Prayer Prompt

God, I celebrate that You are my creator and the author of marriage. I'm so grateful that You've explained Your plan for marriage throughout the Bible (Genesis 2:22–24).

Today, I confess that I have much more to learn about it. I want to be a student of marriage as You created it. I invite your Holy Spirit to teach me the truth and to convict me of my vain notions regarding life as _____'s wife (Psalm 119:105; John 14:26; John 16:8).

I am determined to honor marriage and You, Lord. Help me (Hebrews 13:4).

In Jesus, I pray.

Amen

A Wife's Call to Action

Read over the origin and purpose of marriage in Genesis:

And the LORD God said, It is not good that the man should be alone; I will make a helper for him. . . . But for Adam there was not found a helper fit for him. So the LORD God caused a deep sleep to fall upon the man, and while he slept, took one of his ribs and closed up the place with flesh. And the rib that the LORD God had taken from the man he made into a woman and brought her to the man. Then the man said, "This at last is bone of my bones and flesh of my flesh; she shall be called Woman, because she was taken out of Man." Therefore a man shall leave his father and his mother and hold fast to his wife, and they shall become one flesh (Genesis 2:18–24).

Process that truth with the following questions and comments.

As a wife, what need(s) do you fulfill for your husband?

Take a bold step in preparing to be led by God in your marriage. Grab your husband's hand and pray this prayer or your version of it.

Lord, help me to meet _____'s needs. You have declared that we are one flesh. Help me to express the beauty and glory of that one-flesh relationship with _____.

Chapter 2

You Are a Radiant and Beautiful Bride

Your beauty is a big deal. We all think about it, right? At 45 years old, I am still using concealer to cover up blemishes on my face. While I had hoped for perfect skin, I still face the reality of my imperfect skin. What do you see when you look in the mirror? Do you focus on the imperfections you see? It's hard not to, isn't it? Our minds tend to feast on what we can see. Thankfully, God sees us very differently.

> For the LORD sees not as man sees: man looks on the outward appearance, but the LORD looks on the heart (1 Samuel 16:7).

You are a living in a temporary physical body in an unending spiritual reality. God has given you an earthly beauty and Jesus has secured your spiritual beauty.

Accepting Jesus means you died to sin and became new and one with Him. You are one with the very perfect One. Jesus became a spiritual concealer of your emotional, physical, and spiritual blemishes. You now share His radiance and His inheritance. God looks at you and sees Jesus. All the goodness of Him covers over the best you can do and the worst you will do. In unity with Jesus, you are absolutely radiant.

> Husbands, love your wives, as Christ loved the church and gave himself up for her, that he might sanctify her, having cleansed her by the washing of water with the word, so that he might present the church to himself in splendor, without spot or wrinkle or any such thing, that she might be holy and without blemish (Ephesians 5:25–27).

When you married, you became one with your spouse. You left a life of dependence on your parents. You left a life of independence. You chose a life united with this man until God calls one of you home to heaven. You are no longer your own.

Did you bristle when you read that last line? Before you dig your heels in on this one, give me a second to explain. Unity in marriage is very different than the dependence of a child to a parent. The union of your marriage is a choice to comingle your life goals and choices to include the needs of your spouse. The choice to think of his needs alongside of yours is a beauty treatment for the married soul.

Just as Christ chooses to unite Himself to the church, you have chosen to unite yourself to your spouse. Your unity with Christ will empower your own selfless love — a critical key to loving your husband. As His love radiates through you, you will SHINE! You are the beautiful bride you've hoped to be.

You are enabled by Jesus' Spirit living in you to love him for better or worse, rich or poor, in sickness or in health — the way Jesus has loved you. Because of Jesus, you do not have to earn God's love. Therefore, your husband does not ever have to earn your love. You have chosen to love him as he is. The gift of your steady stream of faithfulness and kindness toward your husband will add to your beauty in ways that you have never imagined.

You may be overwhelmed to think of how much Christ loved you regardless of your faults. You might be nervous, thinking,

"There is no way I'm going to be able to love my husband if he betrays me or hurts me like I've done in my relationship with God."

Do not worry, dear friend. Christ in you means that His power, love, and sound mind have become yours (2 Timothy 1:7). His Spirit lives in you, His radiating beautiful bride, to love your husband. Depend on the One who is love to use your mind, your heart, and your body to love your chosen life mate the way he desires to be loved.

Ahh, and His Spirit is in your husband to love you the way you desire to be loved. Imagine the One who created you and knows you from head to toe, inspiring your husband to love you. God knows your needs better than you do. He will supply your needs out of His enormous love and wealth, and He uses the Holy Spirit of Jesus to do so (Philippians 4:19). God is more committed to you, His radiant bride, than you ever dreamed.

Prayer Prompt

Oh, God, I am trying to absorb this reality of how You see me. I long to see myself the way You do, the radiant bride of Christ (Isaiah 6; 2 Corinthians 11:2).

You know how I think of myself. I surrender it all. Let Your truth guide my thoughts, emotions, and actions. I want my spiritual reality to determine my physical world and especially my marriage (Hebrews 4:13; Ephesians 1:3, 2:22).

I am delighted to be the righteousness of Christ. I want to treat my husband, _____, with the same respect. Help me, Lord (2 Corinthians 5:21; Ephesians 5:33).

In Jesus, I pray.

Amen

A Wife's Call to Action

Choose to Wear White

Wedding etiquette suggests that only a virgin wear a white wedding dress. Jesus has ensured your purity and your white wedding wardrobe.

> He has clothed me with the garments of salvation; he has covered me with the robe of righteousness (Isaiah 61:10).

With a pencil, write three of your big mistakes next to your name on a piece of paper. Thank God for sending Jesus to cover them.

Now erase those mistakes and look at yourself in the mirror and say, "God sees me without those mistakes. Thank You, Jesus!"

Chapter 3

Your Marriage Has an Enemy

When you said "I do" to the faithful, lifelong love commitment of marriage, an enormous bullseye landed on your holy union. While the angels in heaven were rejoicing over your future as one flesh, demons were having committee meetings about how to destroy your happily ever after.

Spiritual warfare is a reality. The horrific things you see on the news are evidence that the war has been going on behind the scenes. The stories of sex trafficking, Christians being imprisoned for their faith, and celebrities whose marriages only last weeks reveal glimpses of the reality. You and I are not immune to the struggle. It's likely you experienced it even before high school.

God has an enemy known as Satan, the devil, the prince of the air, the accuser, the adversary, the prince of darkness, the destroyer, the father of lies, the tempter, and many other names describing his character. He was cast out of heaven for competing with God. He has his own army and there is probably more than one of his troops assigned to you and your Mr. Forever.

Why you? Why marriage?

God's love for you is beautiful, rich, and pure. Satan wants to win the battle against God, so he strikes someone God loves. You've seen it in the movies. The villain who wants to hurt the good guy goes after his family to get his attention! Well, you are the good Guy's family.

The union of marriage is God's design. It's His life-sized illustration of His commitment to love you forever. But it's more than just for your own personal benefit. Your marriage is on display to the rest of your world. As you and your spouse love, honor, and cherish each other, the world sees a reflection of God loving them. But if your commitment to each other is destroyed, what will the world know of God and His enduring, merciful love?

God's enemy wants to shine a dishonorable, untrustworthy light on his opponent. He wants to influence as many people as he can. His goal is to destroy belief in God. He does not get to live in the perfection of heaven and he doesn't want anyone else to either. He wants people shaking their heads in disbelief that God's Word is truth. And he's happy to use you to make it happen.

Think about Potiphar's wife and her attraction to Joseph. When you read Genesis chapter 39, it sounds like she's living the sweet life with everything she could ever want. So why all of a sudden do you think she wanted Joseph? Her pursuit of him was relentless. Did she marry Potiphar planning to cheat on him? I doubt it. What about Joseph? We don't hear any hint of wrongdoing in his character. He represented the character of God, and he enjoyed God's favor. He was a strategic target. Of course, God's enemy would want to try to take him down. It's so messy, isn't it?

That's why I am writing to you. I want you to see the reality behind the divorce statistics. There is a backstory that is as old as Lucifer's fall from heaven. He is a formidable foe. You've seen some of his victories. I saw his destructive nature in my parents' divorce. It opened the door to influence the demise of my first marriage. And it threatened my marriage to David.

To become the radiant, well-armed bride of Christ and that handsome fella you married, you need to see the big picture. You need to know what is at stake and who really loses if you don't show up to fight.

Begin to identify the reality of Satan's war against marriage around you. Let it settle in the front of your mind. You and your husband have an enemy.

God of my marriage, I accept the reality of being a target in the devil's battle against You. I desire Your help in keeping our marriage from becoming a casualty of this war (Ephesians 6:12; Psalm 121:2).

Let Your power and love for me and _____ guide us out of harm's way. Grant us a healthy desire to follow You (2 Timothy 1:7; Psalm 21:1; Deuteronomy 13:4).

We ask this in the name of Jesus.

Amen

A Wife's Call to Action

Review evidence of Satan's attack on marriages in the Bible. Identify Satan's scheme, tactic, and the bigger goal (beyond the immediate relationship) he had in mind. How did he intend to discredit God? I'll give you a head start.

Adam and Eve — Genesis 3

Scheme: Please themselves

Tactic: Ignore God's authority

Big Picture: Cause trouble and hardship for every man and woman. Cause them to question God's goodness toward them.

Uriah and Bathsheba (David's lover) — 2 Samuel 11 & 12

Scheme:

Tactic:

Big Picture:

What others marriages in the Bible were targeted by God's enemy?

Chapter 4

Declare Victory

So, you are in this fight. You know Satan is able to destroy people's lives and marriages. The great news is that God made sure we could enjoy marriage despite the evil one's advances. If you are in Christ, and Christ is in you, you have a very real hope of living victoriously, regardless of the attacks.

We often refer to God as all-powerful, mighty God, victorious warrior, the God of angel armies, and our defender. Over and over again we see God triumphing over darkness in the Bible. The "good news" of the gospel is our greatest evidence of His power and love. We are the walking Bible, living to declare God as victorious to the world.

When God raised Jesus from His burial tomb, our impending death was cancelled. Death is Satan's territory. With the Resurrection of Jesus, God reminds the world that He is the ultimate power. He proved Himself to be more powerful than His opponent. Because Jesus overcame the grave, we can overcome the threat of a dead marriage.

I have said these things to you, that in me you may have peace. In the world you will have tribulation. But take heart; I have overcome the world (John 16:33).

> But thanks be to God, who gives us the victory through
> our Lord Jesus Christ (1 Corinthians 15:57).

The ultimate Bridegroom gave your marriage a fighting chance. I wouldn't be writing to you today if this were not true. My decision to stay married in the midst of my fears and selfish thoughts tempting me to leave was met by God's power. He took my "Yes Lord" and did what I could not do for myself. He moved heaven and earth to help me embrace Jesus' nature and trust it over my own. He delighted to give me the healing and help I needed to thoroughly enjoy this marriage to David. He shepherded me, taught me, and intervened in so many ways. He defends His Bride. You and your husband are His Bride, the Church, and He will fiercely protect your marriage.

John 16:33 confirms that you will have trouble in this world. But Jesus has overcome the world. He is the victorious overcomer! And when you are sure that Jesus is God's Son, then you are a qualified soldier in the fight.

> Who is it that overcomes the world except the one who
> believes that Jesus is the Son of God? (1 John 5:5).

We have a choice. We can fearfully focus on Satan's very real threats and victories — but why would we when we are citizens of heaven, daughters of the King, empowered with God's spirit to overcome? We are on the winning team, living to reveal the win heaven is already celebrating.

Listen to heaven's victory cheer:

> And I heard a loud voice in heaven, saying, "Now the salvation and the power and the kingdom of our God and the authority of his Christ have come, for the accuser of our brothers has been thrown down, who accuses them day and night before our God. And they have conquered him by the blood of the Lamb and by the word of their testimony, for they loved not their lives even unto death. Therefore, rejoice, O heavens and you who dwell in them! But woe to you, O earth and sea, for the devil has come down to you

in great wrath, because he knows that his time is short!" (Revelation 12:10–12).

Heaven is already celebrating your victory in Jesus. Your faith has to partner with the reality of heaven. Faith acts like the many loops made to fit over the buttons on a bridal gown. Each loop secures the dress into place. Every time you speak the truth that Jesus is the way, the truth, and the life for your marriage, your faith is fastened to the reality of heaven.

Prayer Prompt

Thank You, Heavenly Father, for offering the perfect Jesus to save my husband, me, and our marriage. Help me to feel safe, protected in Your presence. Encourage me with the true stories of Your power intervening in marriages. (Hebrews 10:14, Deuteronomy 33:27, Galatians 3:5)

Teach me and _____ to rely on You. Let our testimony of reliance on You be joined with the blood of Jesus to overcome the traps set for us by the evil one. (Psalm 65:5-12, Revelation 12:11)

In the name of Jesus, the ultimate Bridegroom, I pray. Amen

A Wife's Call to Action

Fortify your mind with your spiritual reality by writing heaven's victory cheer in your own words (Revelation 12:10–12).

Declare Revelation 12:11 as your reality. "_____ and I overcome the attacks of the devil by the blood of the Lamb and the sword of the Spirit, God's Word, at work in our lives."

Name one marital issue you can overcome because of Jesus' power at work in you.

Chapter 5

Fight for the Prize

We are at war. We are beautiful Christian women with painted nails and hair products galore, and we are warriors. Before marriage, we were at war as the Bride of Christ. Today, we are the bride of Christ and the bride of another soul fighting this same war. Like it or not, war is our reality.

Many women are good at fighting. But the fight is usually against another person. You've likely been in a fight with your siblings, maybe a parent, and one or two close friends. Take a trip down memory lane back to those events. How did you fight? Was it physical? Were harmful words deployed as weapons? Did you distance yourself from your enemy for hours, days, and maybe years? Was silence your weapon of choice?

Fights can be ugly, right? The wounds are real. Especially if one or more people in the battle are using weapons that are not authorized by God. Yes, God has authorized weapons for you.

> For though we walk in the flesh, we are not waging war according to the flesh. For the weapons of our warfare are not of the flesh but have divine power to destroy strongholds. We destroy arguments and every lofty opinion raised

against the knowledge of God, and take every thought captive to obey Christ (2 Corinthians 10:3–5).

In 2 Corinthians 10:3–4, Paul explains that this is not your great-grandfather's war. The weapons aren't guns, knives, or even nuclear bombs. They are spiritual in nature and provided by God. They have divine power instead of human power. And they are able to destroy strongholds, the places where Satan and his army hide.

According to Paul, these demon-infested fortresses are actually thoughts, lies, and arguments intended to distract people from God and destroy their faith in Him. As a daughter of the King, the bride of Christ, and the wife of your Mr. Forever, your job is to employ God's weapons to tear down these ideas and replace them with God's truth.

The ideas that have to be defeated will come to your mind sounding like your own voice or the voice of someone you highly respect. They might suggest that you deserve better, that you chose the wrong guy, that you are always going to lack the love you desperately need, and so on. They suggest you need to be defended and offer to defend you. They will support the idea of division instead of unity. They will subtly come to you in a steady stream. They will seem harmless and helpful.

One thought I had to learn to resist was, "David isn't the right guy." I heard something similar come from my dad's mouth. And because my dad's opinion was important to me, I listened. This idea about David was man-made, not God-inspired. My mind began to believe the bad press I had heard and it went to work to support the idea. C.S. Lewis explains this well in his book *The Screwtape Letters:* "Suspicion often creates what it suspects."[2]

You must be prepared to fight back by knowing God's character and His will. You need to do the heavy lifting when it comes to honoring marriage and viewing it as worth defending. Then you will be prepared to identify the assaults and referee the internal arguments.

Prayer Prompt

Almighty God, You have provided weapons that are more powerful than I can imagine. Thank You for supplying all my needs and making them available through my relationship with Jesus (2 Corinthians 10:4; Philippians 4:19; Ephesians 1:3).

You alone know the thoughts, lies, and arguments already nesting in my mind and my husband's. Without Your truth, we will suffer at the enemy's hand. Teach us Your truth. Renew our minds by the power of Your Word so that we are not vulnerable to these attacks (Proverbs 5:21; John 8:32; Romans 12:2, 13:14).

Bearing the name of Jesus, I ask these things.

Amen

A Wife's Call to Action

Secure the truth about God's role in your life by writing Zephaniah 3:17 and circling the words that describe God.

The LORD your God is in your midst, a mighty one who will save; he will rejoice over you with gladness; he will quiet you by his love; he will exult over you with loud singing.

Rewrite the verse in your own words, personalizing it with yours and your husband's name.

Find an opportunity to communicate to your husband that no matter what difficulty arises, you are in this battle together and you will always be on his side. It's the two of you and God against anything the enemy can throw against you!

Speaking these truths to your husband will help to establish your own intentions and it will reinforce your unity in marriage.

Chapter 6

The Enemy Exposed

Maybe you are appalled at the thought of having an enemy. Does your heart just long for peace and want everyone to just get along? Me too. For decades, my life revolved around making everyone happy and avoiding conflict. Eventually, I had to grasp the reality that an enemy had been in my life all along. This is true for you, friend. You cannot avoid this enemy. So hunker down, and get to know who and what you are dealing with.

Remember, your enemy is God's enemy. He is a spiritual force that is in direct competition with God. God shows us the motives of His enemy here in Revelation 12:17:

> Then the dragon became furious with the woman and went off to make war on the rest of her offspring, on those who keep the commandments of God and hold to the testimony of Jesus.

Satan, the dragon, is the war maker. Those of us who choose to live by God's instructions are his targets. Our obedience to God brings the blessings Satan will never enjoy. He is angry, jealous, and hoping you will defy God like he did.

He is known as the opposer because he wants to contradict God. You can be sure that his evil army watches and waits for windows of opportunity to suggest a contradiction to the Bible. The Bible tells us exactly who God is and who we are to Him. It tells us how to live, love, and experience the rich life God has ready for us. It is the source of truth, and the enemy of our souls fiercely opposes it.

He and his armies are working double time to hide these facts from you and those who will influence you the most. He wants to skew your idea of God and His truth. Generations of your family have fought this fight. Perhaps some were successful and others not as much. The difference maker is this:

> For to set the mind on the flesh is death, but to set the mind on the Spirit is life and peace (Romans 8:6).

As you reflect on your parents, their parents, and beyond, can you identify stories of peaceful lives and happy marriages? Do you recall accounts of devastation and hopelessness? Each is an indicator of spiritual victories and losses that began in the battlefield of their minds.

But this isn't their marriage, is it? It is yours. You said yes to leaving your family of origin and cleaving (remaining faithful) to your husband. This takes so much thought and determination because our minds naturally agree with what we've seen and heard. Strategically, the war maker exposes you and me to marriage ideas that do not fit into the will of God.

I remember where I was standing in my bedroom when I had this thought. "Everything I learned about marriage from my parents is faulty. I'm 19 years old and I have no foundation for my own good marriage." My next right thought should have been, "But God is for me and He can teach me what I need to know. My parents' mistakes do not have to be my own." But that thought didn't occur to me. I did not have the verse "Nothing will be impossible with God" in my mind to fight off the hopeless feeling that was settling into my soul (Luke 1:37).

Knowing God's Word and His will for marriage are vital to exposing the opposer.

Do not be conformed to this world, but be transformed by the renewal of your mind, that by testing you may discern what is the will of God, what is good and acceptable and perfect (Romans 12:2).

You need to be able to identify the enemy at work around you. You will be able to recognize God's opponent when you know God well. Allow this book to expose you to what God says about you, your spouse, and your marriage. You will recognize your enemy when you know the heart and mind of God and hold everything in comparison to it.

Prayer Prompt

Help me, God! I need You to help me identify the work of the enemy in my life and in my history (Ephesians 1:17).

You are the truth and I desire to live protected by the power and authority of Your Word (John 12:48, 14:6).

You know the words and images in our minds that could destroy the good thing we said yes to. Help us replace them with Your truth (2 Corinthians 10:5; John 8:32).

I want to spend the rest of my marriage relying on You and avoiding the marriage destroyer (Psalm 62:8).

For the sake of our marriage and Your glory, I pray in Jesus' name.

Amen

A Wife's Call to Action

The Bible is where you will discover the difference between God and His enemy. Review and record the five descriptions of God and the five descriptions of Satan I've shared below. Create an opportunity to share them with your husband.

Descriptions of God

1. "The Lord is my Shepherd, I shall not want" (Psalm 23:1).

2. "God is my helper, the Lord is the upholder of my life" (Psalm 54:4).

3. "He gives power to the faint, and to him who has no might he increases strength" (Isaiah 40:29).

4. "God is light, and in him is no darkness at all" (1 John 1:5).

5. "God is love" (1 John 4:8).

Descriptions of Satan

1. Satan disguises himself as an angel of light (2 Corinthians 11:14).

2. Your adversary the devil prowls around like a roaring lion, seeking someone to devour (1 Peter 5:8).

3. "Who accuses them day and night before our God" (Revelation 12:10).

4. "Every spirit that does not confess Jesus is not from God. This is the spirit of the antichrist, which you heard was coming and now is in the world already" (1 John 4:3).

5. He was a murderer from the beginning, and does not stand in the truth, because there is no truth in him. When he lies, he speaks out of his own character, for he is a liar and the father of lies (John 8:44).

Chapter 7

God Is Fighting for You

Throughout the Bible, God confirms to us that He is for us and not against us. The birth, Resurrection, and Second Coming of Jesus are all signs that He is able to protect and save us from this enemy and He wants to. But believing this is key to surviving the skirmishes and celebrating victory.

If God is for us, who can be against us? (Romans 8:31).

I may not know you personally, but I know one thing about you — you have been tempted to believe God does not like you. Life has offered you the opportunity to doubt God will rescue you from something or anything. The father of lies will not fail to orchestrate and influence conversations or events that will lead you (and every other person) to wonder if God smiles when He thinks of you.

In his book *All Is Grace: A Ragamuffin Memoir*, Brennan Manning asks the question:

Do you believe that the God of Jesus loves you beyond worthiness and unworthiness, beyond fidelity and infidelity — that he loves you in the morning sun and in the evening rain — that he loves you when your intellect denies it, your emotions refuse it, your whole being rejects it. Do you believe that God loves without condition or reservation and loves you this moment as you are and not as you should be?[3]

That is a true account of God's love for you, pursuit of you, and faithfulness to you. If it's really hard to believe, you can chalk that up to the work of God's enemy in your life. The more you experience the extravagance of God's love, the less you will allow someone, spiritual being or human, to convince you otherwise.

A.W. Tozer, an author and hero of the Christian faith, rightly explained: "What comes into our minds when we think about God is the most important thing about us."[4] What comes to your mind when you think of God? Do you smile and relax at the thought of Him? Or do you get tense? Do you feel judged, disapproved of, disliked?

Not so many years ago, I was afraid to bow my head to pray. My thoughts of God were not accurate. In my mind, He was mad at me, disappointed in me. Many of the enemy's strategies to keep me from the peace-filled life that God planned for me were working.

My thoughts began to change only after I began to spend almost an hour a day in Bible study. The living Word of God applied to my life for more than the hour or so a week on Sundays made a huge difference. I didn't realize it was happening at the time, but my steady diet on the truth about God changed me. Each time I read His Word, wrote His Word, prayed His Word, I was taking back the land of my mind. I was ripping down the mental wallpaper that kept me from experiencing the reality of God in my life. Knowing more about God and His deep love for me began the healing process from depression, perfectionism, self-hatred, compulsive people pleasing, hyper-self-protection, and husband bashing.

Studying God's names and His roles will supercharge your relationship with Him. It has transformed my prayer life, because I know who I am talking to. One of God's roles in our lives is "mighty warrior." The Bible tells of many battles and how God directed the outcome for those who honored Him as Lord. He is known as Deliverer, Protector, Refuge, and Shepherd. This God has promised to fight for you. He is able to overcome the enemy.

Let these verses encourage you:

Do not be afraid of them, for I am with you to deliver you, declares the LORD (Jeremiah 1:8).

The LORD will fight for you (Exodus 14:14).

The LORD is a man of war; the LORD is his name (Exodus 15:3).

You shall not fear them, for it is the LORD your God who fights for you (Deuteronomy 3:22).

Our God will fight for us (Nehemiah 4:20).

Knowing God is fighting for you can change your approach to marriage. It has changed mine. I am convinced that God is willing and able to help me, and that keeps me from repeating some of the mistakes of my past. Mistakes like panic and knee-jerk reactions. Mistakes like attacking my husband's character based on what I feel or think I see. These are not God's ways.

When you know God is for you and He is mighty to save, you can choose to approach every battle assured of victory. Not because you've got what it takes to make this work out just fine. The battle to love faithfully in the midst of life's randomly occurring heartaches, illness, financial stress, and more is God's.

The battle is not yours but God's (2 Chronicles 20:15).

Prayer Prompt

You are the all-powerful God. There is none like You. I declare that You are for me and not against me. Work in me the confidence I need to act on that truth (Psalm 147:5; Romans 8:31; 2 Corinthians 3:4).

You are mighty to save me from the evil that Satan has planned for me and my marriage. I believe it, but there are also areas in me that doubt it. Would you encourage me? I want to be a bride who consistently relies on You instead of myself (Zephaniah 3:17; Isaiah 41:13).

Because Jesus is my brother and friend, I confidently ask these things of You (Hebrews 2:11; John 15:15).

Amen

❧ A Wife's Call to Action ❧

Read the historical account of Jehoshaphat's battle against the Moabite, Ammonite, and Meunite armies in 2 Chronicles 20.

Jehoshaphat faced a very unfair fight. He was outnumbered. What was his first act of valor in verse 3?

Consider Jehoshaphat one of your battle mentors. Instead of declaring his fears and what could happen, he declared His faith in God as His mighty warrior in 2 Chronicles 20:6. Write your own declaration of faith in God as your mighty warrior using the verses listed in this chapter or find others to support your faith.

Now, start looking for another battle mentor. You need to witness the life of another wife who fights like Jehoshaphat.

Chapter 8

Planning for Victory

You spent months, maybe years, planning your wedding. You dreamed about the wedding day. Every detail was carefully documented. Seriously, just the planning for what you would wear was extensive. But wow, how long did you really get to wear that dress? It was just for a few hours, right? Your investment of time and money on locating and purchasing that dress was quite significant for the hours spent wearing it.

Now, what about the marriage? What are your plans for marriage? Let's say your marriage will last 60-plus years like my mother and father-in-law's. That is almost 526 thousand hours of handholding, chores, laughter, decisions, long kisses, shopping, self-denial, work, etc. Sure, there will be the occasional catered dinner, but the majority of those days and weeks will not be something others will dress up for and plan to celebrate with you.

Have you planned for the rest of your life together? Are you prepared for a 60-year relationship that will be exposed to an ongoing spiritual battle?

If you know God, His unlimited power, and His character, you will trust Him to guide you as Mr. and Mrs. _____. You will study His instructions and act on them. The Spirit of God who lives inside of you will remind you of His Truths and guide you to victory.

> So Jesus said to the Jews who had believed him, "If you abide in my word, you are truly my disciples, and you shall know the truth, and the truth will set you free (John 8:31–32).

Freedom suggests a lack of captivity. God has been very aware of Satan's plan to keep you away from the great life and marriage He designed for you. So He sent Jesus to free everyone who fell for Satan's tactics (Isaiah 61:1). Every husband and every wife can choose captivity or the freedom Jesus offers.

So how do you choose freedom for your life together?

The ticket to remaining faithful and enjoying life together regardless of the enemy's attempts to stop you is this: abiding in Jesus, God's Word made flesh. As you hung on the words of your fiancé, now husband, you were abiding. You were learning "who" he is, and "whose" you would become. But before you were born, you were already promised to Jesus, your spiritual, eternal bridegroom. You said "I do" to Jesus, when you said "yes, I believe Jesus is the Son of God, and the only way to live with God for eternity." Your first abiding is to be with Jesus. Your attention to your eternal love is your priority as a forever bride.

An enduring, love-giving marriage is dependent upon your choice to habitually abide (remain, stay, and continue) in a relationship with Jesus Christ. It includes actively doing what God says to do, modeling Jesus in your conversation and your choices. This ongoing submission to God is, in fact, drawing near to Him. And when we remain in Him or draw near to Him, He promises to show up for us (James 4:8).

One of my friends says Psalm 19:14 to herself before having a discussion with her husband.

> Let the words of my mouth and the meditation of my heart be acceptable in your sight, O LORD, my rock and my redeemer.

She knows that if it is pleasing to the Lord, then surely it will be pleasing to her husband. She said she tried this for a solid weekend and felt like she had gained more control over her words. But she quickly confessed to God that she was still struggling with the meditations of her heart. She planned for her victory by rehearsing God's Word. She made progress and knew it wasn't over. She still needed God's help.

Remember, your mind is where God's enemy plans to attack. It is not something you can turn on and turn off. It is always with you. You are always on the battlefield. Developing an ongoing relationship with God is the only defense you have against Satan's persistent influence and the ungodly desires of your heart.

Knowing specific Scriptures will help you to recognize which of your ideas do not agree with God. You will learn to see the threats and invite God to protect you and your husband. God provides for all of our needs and that includes the armor necessary to defend our thoughts.

This book is written for you, the wife. You are responsible for abiding in Jesus and relying on Him to guide you to the finish line in marriage. Your husband has the same responsibility. Together you can plan to finish well under the authority of the overcomer.

More Jesus, more victory. Less Jesus, less victory.

Prayer Prompt

I want to abide, God. I want to remain, to continue in my relationship with You through Your Word. Empower me to draw near to You. Guide me away from trusting myself and the many options presented to me by the world. Help my husband to desire the same abiding in You (John 15:4; James 4:8; Proverbs 3:5–6).

Without Your help, I will be a rebellious bride, falling for the lies, distractions, and schemes Satan has planned. With Your help, I will be safe (Zephaniah 3:2; Psalm 54:4).

Renew my desire to lean on You. I am so grateful that Your love for me and _____ offers us freedom from the destruction the enemy wants to cause in our marriage (Psalm 37:3; Galatians 5:1; John 10:10).

In Jesus' name, I ask for Your help.

Amen

A Wife's Call to Action

Answer this question: Have I planned for an amazing marriage as well as I planned for an incredible wedding?

Compared to your wedding day, what value would you place on your marriage? If your wedding was worth $10,000, your marriage is worth what?

Schedule a "Let's Invest in Our Marriage" meeting with your husband. Together you can begin to create a strategy to keep your vows.

Chapter 9

Your Marching Orders: Show Up, Surrender, and Salute

You may feel weak and unprepared for a 60-year war. But friend, your leader is not weak or unprepared. He has already sealed the victory.

> But thanks be to God, who gives us the victory through our Lord Jesus Christ (1 Corinthians 15:57).

You are a soldier (a beautiful one) enlisted in God's army. In order to survive each battle, you MUST trust the One giving the orders. Trust happens over a period of time. As you show up for training (Bible study, worship, Scripture memorization, etc.), you learn to surrender your "great ideas" and go with the expert's plan. You receive your orders, and salute the One who gave them to you. Your salute says, "You are the Boss. All eyes are on You. I am here and ready to be led by You, God."

Imagine a scenario where you are physically sick, constantly getting worse and going to the doctor for tests. After days, weeks, or maybe even years of appointments and testing, you discover you have stage four cancer. You have no idea when your body became a battleground for this cancer. You didn't know that little symptom was a sign you would one day fight for your life. Had you known in advance that the cancer was coming, you would have sought out the expert immediately. You would have consulted with this doctor and followed his or her instructions to the T. You would have done anything to avoid the pain of surgery, chemo, radiation, sickness, and maybe death.

There were several years in my marriage to David that I wandered away from God's leadership.

As issues between David and me surfaced, I began to limp spiritually. I knew I was limping, but I couldn't put my finger on why. I ignored the limp and kept smiling, kept cooking, and enjoying his company most of the time. Each time a problem arose for us, the pain multiplied. Pretty soon it was obvious I was hurting by the scowl on my face, and the tone of my voice. I was unaware of the spiritual battle that was taking place behind the scenes. I evaluated the situation and concluded, marriage hurt. I surmised that since I was married to David, my pain must be his fault.

I didn't know my marriage limp could turn into the potential amputation of my spouse. I didn't know to seek the expert in advance of this problem. I had no knowledge of His expertise in this area or His willingness to treat me. Because of this, I nearly chose to walk away from another marriage.

Our marriage is alive and well because we chose to act on wisdom that fell in line with God's instructions. We took chance after chance that His way would be more productive than our own. God did not require perfection from us the way you imagine a platoon captain inspecting the company's barracks. Both of us would fail miserably at the white glove relationship test. In our own ways, we showed up to do what biblical counselors and leaders were teaching us to do. We were drawing near to God, and He in turn showed up to do more than we could ask or imagine.

You have the same victorious outcome ahead of you. You are destined to be a lifelong bride when you and your husband surrender your ideas and strategies to God's. Your role is to join the right army, confident of its leader's battle plan.

Let my testimonies of God's faithfulness in part two of this book encourage you to show up for this battle on God's side. I've written Scripture-based prayers for you that will arm you with God's truth and help you to continue to abide in Him.

God provides the weapons and the strategies you need to outlast the assaults awaiting you. Remember, what you wear to the marriage matters so much more than what you wore to the wedding. In Jesus, you are always a beautiful bride wearing white. You are fighting in God's army to let the world know that He is always faithful to His Word. Your thriving marriage will reflect His faithful love to the world around you when you and your husband allow God to rule.

Prayer Prompt

God, I am showing up to this battle as Your soldier. I surrender my preconceived plans for success in marriage, and salute You as my ultimate authority (2 Timothy 2:3; 2 Chronicles 20:6).

With You, I will fight for my marriage and not against it. Thank You for Your willingness and Your ability to protect me and my husband from the enemy (Psalm 91:2).

Be our guide, our hiding place, our fortress, our faithful protector (Psalm 18:2).

In the name of Jesus, I pray.

Amen

A Wife's Call to Action

Look at your favorite picture of you in your wedding gown. Use your imagination to see yourself in that gown saluting God as the ultimate decision-maker in your marriage. What emotion do you experience? Are you nervous? Do you feel relief, or something in between? Is there a little reservation in your salute? Maybe you are wondering if this is necessary.

God knows what is in your heart. He already knows about your pride, your fear, your self-confidence, and your experiences with authorities. Regardless of those things, He is prepared to empower you to do it anyway.

Daniel modeled for you and me a brave choice to honor God as His authority. He made an unpopular decision to pray to God regardless of King Darius's edict to seek his favor and no other gods (Daniel 6). The consequences of doing so meant a trip to the lion's den. It looked like a bad decision until God shut the mouths of the lions and showed Himself to be in charge!

That is the God of your marriage. Always victorious in the lives of those who show up, surrender, and salute Him as their authority.

Go to PrayersforNewBrides.com/chapter9 to read the true accounts of three wives who chose to follow God's orders for marriage instead of a well-respected voice of reason.

Your Armor, Ma'am

To be prepared for war is one of the most effectual means of preserving peace.[5]

— General George Washington

Prayer is not the preparation for the battle, it is the battle.[6]

— Jennifer Smith, *The Unveiled Wife*

Chapter 10

The Dress Code for Battle

As the bride of Christ, and the wife of _____, you are going to make a fashion statement. The world is ready for a bride who wears white, but they might stare awhile at an armored wife. This is not your average wedding wardrobe. But you are not average. You are royalty, daughter of the King of kings. Maybe you didn't get the designer wedding dress you wanted. But God, the designer of your life, created you with great plans to protect you.

The dress code for victorious living and life together is found in Ephesians chapter 6. Consider it your invitation to success in the battle to remain married. I'm breaking it down line by line for you because each line is critically important.

> [10]Finally be strong in the Lord and in the strength of his might.
>
> [11]Put on the whole armor of God that you may be able to stand against the schemes of the devil.
>
> [12]For we do not wrestle against flesh and blood, but against the rulers, against the authorities, against the cosmic powers over this present darkness, against the spiritual forces of evil in the heavenly places.

¹³Therefore take up the whole armor of God, that you may be able to withstand in the evil day, and having done all, to stand firm.

¹⁴Stand therefore, having fastened on the belt of truth, and having put on the breastplate of righteousness,

¹⁵and, as shoes for your feet, having put on the readiness given by the gospel of peace.

¹⁶In all circumstances take up the shield of faith, with which you can extinguish all the flaming darts of the evil one;

¹⁷and take the helmet of salvation, and the sword of the Spirit, which is the word of God,

¹⁸praying at all times in the Spirit, with all prayer and supplication. To that end keep alert with all perseverance, making supplication for all the saints,

The great news about your new wardrobe is that you can shop the Bible for the rest of your life to add to your collection. There will be no going-out-of-style worries for you. Every item you find will complement the other. And the bonus: the longer you have it, the more valuable and beautiful it becomes.

The **Belt of Truth** is the first essential piece. Stop thinking about your waistline, okay? This belt is different. The belt, God's Word, is necessary to hold all the other armor in place. The only way to know if you are being lied to is to know God's truth. The truth is packed into the Bible. Anyone vulnerable to the enemy attack, especially you and your marriage, will be protected by knowing God as He is revealed to us throughout the Bible.

> The LORD is near to all who call on him, to all who call on him in truth (Psalm 145:18).

The **Breastplate of Righteousness** is the lifestyle of godliness, otherwise known as obedience to God. This is the life modeled for us by Jesus, God's Son. Jesus' sinless life was the ransom paid for you to be one with God, empowered by His Spirit, and able to resist temptation. Knowing God's Word enables us to act accordingly. The breastplate covers the heart and matters of the heart.

> And the effect of righteousness will be peace, and the result of righteousness, quietness and trust forever (Isaiah 32:17).

The **Shoes of Peace** give you a freedom to move forward facing the battle without the distraction of looking down to see what could hinder your next step. With knowledge of God's character and commands found in the Bible, you will trust that living His way is right and safe. This peace will enable you to stand up and keep moving as you trek across the battlefield. Stilettos are not required!

> You keep him in perfect peace whose mind is stayed on you, because he trusts in you (Isaiah 26:3).

The **Shield of Faith** must be worn to defend against the doubts that Satan, the prince of the air, will launch toward you like flaming arrows. Imagine yourself in a great raincoat and matching umbrella, ready for the rain. The shield of faith defends your mind from the doubts, lies, and "what if's" that Satan is great at using against you. Knowing who God is because you have invested time in His Word will strengthen your faith. Each time you place your trust in His love for you and His ability to protect you, your faith in Him will shield your mind and heart. You grab the raincoat and umbrella when rain is in the forecast. Do the same with your faith. Expect the flaming darts to come at you and your husband. Stand ready lift up your shield of faith to defend yourself.

> He grew strong in his faith as he gave glory to God, fully convinced that God was able to do what he had promised (Romans 4:20–21).

The **Helmet of Salvation** is yours as the bride of Christ. Helmets are protective. You are in Christ, wearing the protective covering of His perfection. The Holy Spirit resides within you and can act as a force field to the ideas that could result in you missing God's well-planned good life for you. Remember, our enemy uses lies to destroy people's futures and marriages. Having the mind of Christ gives you the protection you need to continue living according to God's truth.

> For the weapons of our warfare are not of the flesh but have divine power to destroy strongholds. We destroy arguments and every lofty opinion raised against the knowledge of God, and take every thought captive to obey Christ (2 Corinthians 10:4–5).

> "For who has understood the mind of the Lord so as to instruct him?" But we have the mind of Christ (1 Corinthians 2:16).

The name of Jesus sends our enemy to his knees, making way for the power of Jesus. You can wear the name of Jesus as you enjoy His Spirit teaching you to act on the mind of Christ.

The **Sword of the Spirit, which is the Word of God**! By now, you are seeing the protective nature of this wardrobe. God's Word is the thread woven through each important piece.

The Sword, God's Word, is an offensive weapon (think Taser gun) while the others are protective. Jesus spoke words from the Bible when being tempted by Satan. He didn't just remember them. He spoke the truth out loud. Each time He replied to Satan with the words "It is written." Who won that battle? Jesus, who had not eaten for 40 days, defeated Satan. The evil one had no effective defense against God's Word.

> Death and life are in the power of the tongue, and those who love it will eat its fruits (Proverbs 18:21).

Praying the Words of God has been an incredible force for healing in my life and marriage. God watches over His Word to accomplish what it says (Jeremiah 1:12). I have literally spoken God's truth and watched it eventually become my reality.

We are familiar with the concept, "You are what you eat." Well, you are saved, you have faith, you are righteousness, and you have peace because you have dined on the truth. Your heart and mind toward your spouse and your marriage will be as healthy as the information you put into your mind and speak from your mouth. You have to decide where you will shop for your words. What will you choose to feed yourself? You have the opportunity to feed the Spirit living in you with words of life. Doing so will starve your sin nature that wants to live under its own authority instead of God's.

This spiritual armor is invisible in this physical world, just like our God. We are all spiritual beings living in a physical world. The Bible, our one true history, assures us that this world and its desires will pass away. But the one who does the will of God never ceases to exist with Him (1 John 2:17).

If nurtured, your relationship with the unseen God will become more vibrant and real. The same will happen with the unseen armor He provides you. The unchanging God is always available and ready to lead you to victory. You have an active role in the victory. You must suit up in the armor only He provides.

Prayer Prompt

Lord and Commander, You are the all-mighty and victorious God. You are also my Defender and Supplier of all my needs (Joshua 5:14; 1 Corinthians 15:57; Psalm 18:1; Philippians 4:19).

Thank You for the gift of a relationship with You. You are my shield, offering me protection from the enticements the enemy offers. You have armed me with all that is needed to be victorious in life and in my marriage (Psalm 28:7; Ephesians 6:13–18).

Hear my grateful heart praising You for Your incredible love that protects me. Teach me, Lord, to incorporate this armor into my every thought, feeling, word, and action (Psalm 3:3; John 14:26).

I am in awe of You (Psalm 33:8).
With the mighty name of Jesus, I pray.
Amen

A Wife's Call to Action

Swing your sword by praying God's Word back to Him. I'll get you started.

I am the bride of Christ. Jesus covers me with His righteousness (Ephesians 5:27).

God arms me with strength and trains me for battle (Psalm 18:32, 34).

It's your turn. Write and recite your own, based on these verses:

2 Corinthians 10:4
Ephesians 6:11

Chapter 11

Your Posture Matters

How is your posture? Are you a slumper, sloucher, or an abs-tight, stand-up-straight kind of girl? Our thoughts about ourselves and the hope we have for a great life are often reflected in our posture. The thought of being a bride seems to give every woman a pep in her step and a square to her shoulders. There are no slouching brides featured in the magazines.

What happens to your posture when you hear these words:

> God's name is your protection. As you live under His authority you live under the authority and power of His name. This brings all in heaven, on earth, and under the earth to their knees. The authority of Jesus' name trumps Satan's authority and renders him in a humble position — on his knees. (See Proverbs 18:10; Philippians 2:10.)

I hope that you are more than just a little excited that you bear the name that sends Satan to his knees. I feel taller and stronger just typing the words! We have reason to be confident in our role as the bride of Christ and the wife of our Mr. Faithful.

Ephesians chapter 6 specifically instructs us to have a standing posture in this spiritual battle.

[11]Put on the whole armor of God, that you may be able to *stand* against the schemes of the devil.

[13]Therefore take up the whole armor of God, that you may be able to withstand in the evil day, and having done all, to *stand* firm.

Imagine fighting a war sitting down. Seems like a ridiculous idea, right? Your fight for your marriage is not something you can put on hold while you pursue some other honorable mission. Sitting down on this job is not an option. A mighty force will plow you down if you do not follow the instructions of the only One who has the power to defeat the enemy.

God tells us to STAND.

Standing as an armored bride in a spiritual battle for your marriage means holding your position. It is a courageous stance proclaiming that you are confident in the One fighting for you. As you stand, you are exercising your faith in Jesus to not only defeat Satan, but to also strengthen you to endure the attack.

The goal is to stand without wavering or falling. As wives, we are to strive to live in agreement with God. This is a life lived in submission to Him. It means rejecting what we think we "want" and what we "feel" when it does not agree with His Word.

> Submit yourselves therefore to God. Resist the devil, and he will flee from you (James 4:7).

Do you see where standing firm fits into resisting the devil? Stand firm on what God says, who He is, and what He can do. Resist the temptation to agree with anything else. And the devil will flee from you. Persevere. You must endure the battle, trusting that God is able to defeat the enemy and empower you to remain standing.

Remember, God is not sitting on the throne evaluating your ability to stand in hopes that you make it this time. He is actively involved in helping you stand. He has an unlimited supply of time, wisdom, strength, and love for you. He empowers you to stand.

Paul prays for believers to be strengthened by His power in their inner being (Ephesians 3:17). I am praying that for you. You can pray that for yourself. God has the resources to do it. All you have to do is ask. The same power that raised Jesus from the dead lives inside your mind and body to help you stand up to the storms that will surely happen in your married life.

Prayer Prompt

God, I am completely relying on You to prepare me to stand up to the hard days in my marriage. I have no idea what is ahead of us. My faith for our future is in Your ability to protect us, to save us from ourselves and other obstacles (Isaiah 26:4; Jeremiah 17:6–8; 2 Thessalonians 3:3).

I commit to standing under Your leadership and following Your commands (Joshua 5:14).

In Jesus' name, I pray.

Amen

A Wife's Call to Action

On a scale from 1 to 10, where do you land on the subject of standing under God's leadership regardless of the circumstances? One is where you crumble under any pressure to be like the rest of the people in your life. Ten could be you praying aloud with a friend in a public arena other than a Christian event.

Here is an exercise you can use to move your number up the scale and strengthen your ability to remain on God's side of the battle.

Find one person who is willing to pray with another person in a secular crowd and interview them. Here are a few questions to get you started.

- When did your faith in God become so real that other people's opinions of you stopped mattering?

- What battles have you faced that God used to show you He is more powerful than His evil enemy?
- What story in the Bible gives you courage and why?
- What Bible verses do you pray over yourself?

After the interview, reevaluate your willingness to pray with someone publicly. Did your number improve?

Put yourself to the test. Will you look for an opportunity to stand under God's authority this week? Ask God for one.

Chapter 12

Communicate with Your Commander

Have you been a shy communicator when it comes to talking to God? Perhaps you are already praying all the time. Maybe you are somewhere in between, like me. Your prayer life, like mine, is a real battlefield. Satan, who does not want you to be helped by God, is ready to exploit your doubts, fears, insecurities, and bad experiences to his advantage. Your confidence in God is a huge threat to Satan's plan to distract people from God.

Prayer is simply talking to God and listening, too. It is the privilege of communicating with the Creator and sustainer of the universe. Imagine sitting at a table in the local coffee shop with God. He's the most powerful force in the entire world, and yet there He is talking to you.

How did this happen? Jesus did this for you. He reserved your seat at this table. Believing Jesus did this for you opens the door for you to be a friend of God. Praying, or communicating with God, is as simple as developing an intimate friendship with the One who loves perfectly and has all the riches, honor, and power.

Prayer initiates change. Presenting God with a need, a question, or a hope invites God into an active role in your life, in your world.

Nothing is impossible for God. He delivers more than we can ask or imagine. E.M. Bounds says, "God shapes the world by prayer. The more praying there is in the world the better the world will be, the mightier the forces against evil."[7] Your conversations with God can shape the world! Your prayers are mighty against the forces of evil! Isn't that motivating?

Can anything keep your prayers from being fruitful and effective?

Yes, ma'am! You and I have the power to render all of our prayers useless when we ask for something that is out of God's will, ask with wrong motives, ignore God's instructions, and refuse to confess our sins (1 John 5:14; James 4:3; Psalm 66:18; Proverbs 28:9). That is a VERY important list.

Here's the deal. We are always going to need God's forgiveness for falling out of sync with His kingdom's culture. We are simple humans who miss the mark. In battle, we sometimes fall for the sneak attack. Admitting our faults endears us to God. Listen to this, friend:

> If my people who are called by my name humble themselves, and pray and seek my face and turn from their wicked ways, then I will hear from heaven and will forgive their sin and heal their land (2 Chronicles 7:14).

We keep praying, seeking God's help as we turn away from the thing that is separating us from the blessing God wants to give, the healing He is ready to offer. We will always need to confess our shortcomings. Everyone does.

Be warned, the deceiver will suggest to you that God will not accept your confession. And maybe he will suggest it's too small to worry about confessing. He will encourage you to hide the truth from everyone, especially God. Your defense to that sneak attack is this statement:

> "This man, Jesus, receives sinners and eats with them" (Luke 15:2).

When we struggle to know how to pray as a means of defending ourselves against the evil one, we can pray the Word the way Jesus did. As you say the words of truth, in the spiritual realm the sword of the spirit is slicing the slimy tentacles of sin away from you.

The list of approved weapons in our battle against the marriage destroyer ends with prayer. We are invited to be "praying at all times in the Spirit, with all prayer and supplication. To that end keep alert with all perseverance, making supplication for all the saints" (Ephesians 6:18).

I encourage you to seek out additional resources on prayer. This book will surely not cover it to the depths that it deserves. I am a student of prayer and I would love for you to join me on the journey. My words to you are just a glimpse into the most powerful and fulfilling relationship you can ever have.

Prayer Prompt

God, I am in awe that You desire to communicate with me. Thank You for always being with me and attentive to me (Jeremiah 33:3; Psalm 41:10; Genesis 28:15).

Teach me to pray. My desire is to hear Your voice and follow Your instructions (Luke 11:1; John 10:27).

I want to live humbly at Your feet, acknowledging and relying on Your power and Your goodness. Help me to push past the internal and spiritual resistance to talk to You (Luke 10:39; 1 Peter 5:6; Matthew 26:41).

In the name of Jesus, I ask these things of You
Amen

A Wife's Call to Action

To live an effective praying life, you need to be comfortable confessing your sin. Confession is a form of prayer that surprisingly opens the door to great relief. It just takes a little practice to push past the fear.

I'll go first. "God, it's hard to admit, but it's true. At times, I find myself dismissing my husband's ideas. The meditations of my heart are a mess. I confess to You that I am guilty of not respecting my husband. Please forgive me. I want to be completely obedient to You in this area. I need Your help."

Okay. Your turn.

Part 2

Preparing for Victory

You are a radiant bride. You are living united as one with your chosen husband. Your life together is responsible for reflecting Christ's covenant of love with His people. You are in a relationship with the Almighty God. He is the victorious warrior and defender of marriages. He will prepare you for every battle against division and divorce.

God, your Master and Commander, is a very generous Provider. He promises that if you ask, He will answer.

> Ask, and it will be given to you; seek, and you will find; knock, and it will be opened to you. For everyone who asks receives, and the one who seeks finds, and to the one who knocks it will be opened (Matthew 7:7–8).

Jesus taught us to pray for life on earth to be as it is in heaven (Matthew 6:10). Imagine what your marriage looks like in heaven! Everything that is needed for God's plan for your marriage to happen on earth is available to you and _____. With His death and resurrected life, Jesus put your names on all the resources of heaven.

But asking God for His help takes humility. Asking admits your human limitations and need for help. I know from experience that God will strengthen you and your marriage when you ask Him to intervene.

> If you then, who are evil, know how to give good gifts
> to your children, how much more will the heavenly Father
> give the Holy Spirit to those who ask him! (Luke 11:13).

In part two of this book, the focus is on recognizing the schemes of the enemy and praying God's Word. Knowing God, interacting with Him through His Word, asking Him to fulfill His promises, and doing what His Word says to do will strengthen your armor and better equip you for victory.

Praying for yourself is critical to remaining your husband's beautiful bride. Remember the flight attendant's safety instructions? Put on your oxygen mask first and then help the people next to you.

Becoming a wife who bears all things, believes all things, hopes all things, and endures all things takes God's supernatural intervention. What you will need to remain in a love-giving relationship with your husband is not a mystery to God. He has perfect knowledge and a calendar of your life filled out with every detail. He is ready to prepare you for victory. God Gives!

Heaven lacks no good thing and neither should your husband. Interceding for him is a history-changing act of love. Praying for him is simply drawing near to God on his behalf.

As his wife, you have earned a front row seat to his spiritual battle. You will witness the blows to his ego, the doubts, the temptations, and devastations. You will see his successes, his temptations to coast, to rely on himself, and to work for the world's applause.

Jesus sees it from your perspective and God's. He knows exactly what God is capable of doing to guide, defend, correct, and protect your husband. He is seated next to God interceding for your man (Romans 8:34), and He invites you to join Him in the work of prayer.

God Gives!

Interceding for your marriage is similar to registering for your wedding. But it is better. Heaven is filled with all that we need to live with God and in service to Him forever. We don't have to buy it or ask someone to get it for us. Jesus took care of that. We have access to it all.

> Blessed be the God and Father of our Lord Jesus Christ, who has blessed us in Christ with every spiritual blessing in the heavenly places (Ephesians 1:3).

When we pray for our marriage, we are communicating with the One who designed it. Don't forget His Son is married to the Church, which has to be way more complex than your situation. We trust that He will understand it better than we do, and we rely on Him to joyfully take the thing we need off the shelf of heaven and deliver it to us here on earth.

Prayer, your interaction with the One true God, will prepare you for marriage.

Each time He intervenes, you will witness His character and abilities. Your faith will multiply as you rely on Him and see Him at work. You see His hand at work and your heart will soar knowing you got to see His love in action for you. You will feel more comfortable with Him and more freedom to ask for His help. You will trust Him. You will be confident that He is working behind the scenes to pour out the wealth of heaven to meet your needs.

Your armor will be as natural to you as the sound of your name. His truth, His righteousness, His peace, His faith, His salvation, and His sword will be yours.

> The young lions suffer want and hunger; but those who seek the LORD lack no good thing (Psalm 34:10).

Basic Training: Becoming a Forever Bride

Happily ever after is not a fairy tale. It's a choice.[8]

— Fawn Weaver

Choose this day whom you will serve (Joshua 24:15).

Chapter 13

Know God and Trust Him to Defend You

Do you know God?

If you had asked me in my first marriage and the beginning of this marriage, I would have answered, "Of course!" I grew up in a Baptist church. I attended Sunday school, Training Union, church camp, and sang in the choir when I was old enough. I started a Fellowship of Christian Students in our high school and attended a Baptist college. How could I not know God?

Somewhere in my journey of counseling and Bible study I realized I had been "people pleasing" God, too. I began to see that I was trying to be good enough to keep Him from being disappointed with me. My view of God was smudged by my own insecurities. I had read and heard God is love, but my heart did not apply that truth. I suppose my brain filed it under "good to know."

One day I was reading 1 Corinthians 13 and hearing myself read the words, "Love is patient, Love is kind." Suddenly I knew that God was patient and kind. Where had I been? The factoids of "God is love," and "God loves you" suddenly meant, "God is patient and kind with you, Jennifer!" The window of my heart finally had a few less smudges. I was finally seeing glimpses of who God truly is. And I was so relieved.

Knowing God better enabled me to experience His love. It settled my soul. Once my settled soul began to receive true love from God, I was able to give love to David. My energy was no longer tied up in defending my worth and measuring it based on my husband's words or actions.

My obsession with getting love and being loved had been met. Then and only then was I able to give to and serve my husband without manipulative motives or a grumbling spirit.

God will gladly answer your prayer to know the reality of who He is. His truth will remove the lies you didn't know you believed about Him and yourself. I am celebrating the victory that will follow as you pray the following prayer and those His Spirit prompts you to pray.

May His Word erase all the smudges on the windows of your heart, and may you find peace knowing God is your defender.

Prayer Prompt

Father, I desire to know more about You, Your Son, and Holy Spirit (Jeremiah 9:23–24).

I stretch out my hands toward You, reaching for Your Spirit of wisdom and revelation. Take me by the hand and lead me to the truth of who You are. Highlight the chapters and verses of Your Word that will help me to experience Your love for me, my husband, and others (Ephesians 1:17; 2 Thessalonians 3:5).

Engrave Your Word on my mind and heart so that it is a permanent part of me. I invite Your Holy Spirit to fuel a passion within me for Your Word and truth that will increase each day and never be extinguished (Matthew 16:15–16; Jeremiah 31:33–34; Hosea 6:3).

Thank You for the transforming power of Your Word that will change me into who You created me to be. Replace every distorted idea I have of who You are with Your truth. Your Word is my defense against Satan's lies and schemes set to destroy me and my marriage (Romans 12:2; 2 Corinthians 10:5; Ephesians 6:17).

Work in me a desire to know You more than I want fame, wealth, and anything else the enemy uses to distract me. Knowing You is my highest priority (Matthew 6:33).

Knowing You will help me to submit to You as Lord. With You as my Lord, I will have nothing to fear (Isaiah 6:1–9; Psalm 118:6; 2 Timothy 1:7).

In the name of Jesus, I offer my prayer to You, God. Amen

⌒ A Wife's Call to Action ⌒

How much energy are you spending defending yourself? Do you mentally argue your own defense or are you a very verbal defender of your worth and rights?

The Bible says God is your defender. The Psalmist relates to God as his shield, his defender, his stronghold, and his refuge in times of need.

Personalize the following verses so you can be more at ease knowing God is your defender.

> Psalm 7:9–10
> Psalm 18:2, 20
> Psalm 91:1–2

Reread Daniel chapter 6 and experience God as Daniel's defense in the lion's den.

Take a few minutes to journal your thoughts about God as your defender and the defender of your marriage.

Chapter 14

See Yourself through God's Eyes

What if you inherited $68 million but you couldn't take possession of it until you turned 75 years old? You'd be rich, right? But you would have to wait a long time to live rich.

You struggled all of those years but you knew there was hope. And finally the day you had dreamed of arrives. You show up at the attorney's office to collect your grand inheritance on your 75th birthday.

The new secretary would greet you with a big smile because she knew this was the BIG day. But she has just one question. Why hadn't you been living on the interest all of these years?

Interest? What? Your mind races through the scrapbook of your last few decades imagining what that interest could have changed for you and your whole family. You sigh, thinking, "How could I have not known?"

When I said yes to Jesus, I knew that heaven with Jesus was in my future. I knew that heaven was going to be a sweeter life than this one. But I did not notice my everyday living being radically different than before Jesus.

Fast forward to the counseling session where I was introduced to the list entitled "Who I am in Christ." That list is the interest on my inheritance. And it is yours too.

Saying yes to Jesus changed my spiritual identity. I gained all the privileges of being in God's family. God adopted me. Jesus bought that privilege for me with His life. But I spent years living as if I were an orphan with a promise of a good life one day. It sounds absurd, doesn't it?

The truth was in the Bible and I had been reading it. But I needed more understanding, more teaching. Words can't express my thankfulness to God for delivering this truth to me.

I am much more to God than I ever dreamed possible. I have a spiritual reality that changes my earthly life and lifestyle. You do too.

You and I have an enemy who does not want us to know who we are to God and how much He loves us. It is likely that he has worked diligently to make sure you are not aware of who you are to the Creator and Redeemer of your soul. But he loses! The interest on the inheritance is yours!

Faith in this God-given reality of yours will make a huge difference in your sacred marriage. Believing you are accepted, secure, and significant will catapult your confidence. With a confident heart, you will approach your life together with a peace the world does not understand.

Do not wait any longer to live on the interest of this incredible spiritual inheritance.

It is yours!

Prayer Prompt

Father, Your Word tells me that You knew me before I was born. You created me and planned a life of hope for me in advance. I believe that as my Creator, You see the real me. You know me better than I know myself (Jeremiah 1:5; Psalm 139:16).

I want to see myself as You see me. I want to agree with Your thoughts about me so that I become the woman and wife You designed me to be. Break down the walls of fear and pride that keep me from knowing who I became when I embraced Jesus' sacrificial love on the Cross (Isaiah 6:1–6; Proverbs 29:23; Ephesians 2:13).

I invite Your Holy Spirit to convict me of any sin that I have committed that separates me from the full knowledge of You and my place in Your family (John 16:8; Isaiah 59:2; Colossians 1:21).

I choose to put on the truth. I have a new wardrobe, the clothing of a daughter of the Most High, the King of kings (Ephesians 6:10–17; Isaiah 61:10; Psalm 45:13).

A Wife's Call to Action

Read the list below that describes who you are because of Jesus.

Take time to write out the Scripture verse and your own thoughts regarding your identity based on that Scripture.

You may find yourself doubting some of these facts are true about you. That is evidence that Satan has been successful at distorting your thoughts about yourself. I doubted many of them in the beginning. It took prayer, saying these facts out loud, time, and experience for me to overcome the doubts I had.

Dig into this truth. Don't miss living out your spiritual inheritance on this earth and in this marriage.

I AM ACCEPTED:
I am God's child. John 1:12
I am Christ's friend. John 15:15
I have been justified. Romans 5:1
I am united with the Lord and one with Him in spirit. 1 Corinthians 6:17

I have been bought with a price . . . I belong to God. 1 Corinthians 6:20

I am a member of Christ's body. 1 Corinthians 12:27

I am a new creation. 2 Corinthians 5:17

I am a saint. Ephesians 1:1

I have been adopted as God's child. Ephesians 1:5

I have direct access to God through the Holy Spirit. Ephesians 2:18

I have been redeemed and forgiven of all my sins. Colossians 1:14

I am complete in Christ. Colossians 2:10

I AM SECURE:

I am free from condemnation. Romans 8:1–2

I am assured that all things work together for good. Romans 8:28

I am free from any condemning charges against me. Romans 8:31–34

I cannot be separated from the love of God. Romans 8:35–39

I have been established, anointed, and sealed by God. 2 Corinthians 1:21–22

I am hidden with Christ in God. Colossians 3:3

I am confident that the good work that God has begun in me will be perfected. Philippians 1:6

I am a citizen of heaven. Philippians 3:20

I have not been given a spirit of fear, but of power, love, and a sound mind. 2 Timothy 1:7

I can find grace and mercy in time of need. Hebrews 4:16

I am born of God, and the evil one cannot touch me. 1 John 5:18

I AM SIGNIFICANT:

I am the salt and light of the earth. Matthew 5:13

I am a branch of the true vine, a channel of His life. John 15:1, 5

I have been chosen and appointed to bear fruit. John 15:16

I am a personal witness of Christ's. Acts 1:8

I am God's temple. 1 Corinthians 3:16

I am a minister of reconciliation. 2 Corinthians 5:18–20

I am God's coworker. 2 Corinthians 6:1

I am seated with Christ in the heavenly realm. Ephesians 2:6

I am God's workmanship. Ephesians 2:10

I may approach God with freedom and confidence. Ephesians 3:12

I am chosen of god, holy and dearly loved. Colossians 3:12

I am one of God's living stones and am being built up (in Christ) as a spiritual house. 1 Peter 2:5

I can do all things through Christ who strengthens me. Philippians 4:13[9]

Chapter 15

See Your Spouse through God's Eyes

How do you see your husband? What do you see in him? What do you hope for him?

Do you look at him and see the one who will fulfill your every need? Bill payer? Listener? Heart-mender?

When he speaks to you, do you hear his interests? His hopes and dreams?

When you hope for something for your husband, is it that he will change, be more _____, or less _____? Do you hope for a better job for him? Do you wish he could be a better _____?

Do you think about him the way your mom thinks of your dad? Have you usurped her "these characteristics = good husband" mindset? What about your married girlfriends? Have you decided a husband is who your friend says her husband is?

I hate to admit it, but the man I married has been the victim of comparison and of my imagination. But the truth is, I married a unique person, one of God's unrepeated masterpieces. I said "I do" to enjoying this incredible creation for the rest of my life.

Who does *God* say your husband is?

Your husband is a work in progress. He is not perfect. But he has been rescued from being a slave to sin. When he said yes to Jesus, he became a royal subject of the King of the universe. You are married to royalty! (*If your husband is not yet a Christ follower, you can be certain that God wants that for him. God will use you to display the beautiful life God is offering him.*)

Perhaps he is not acting like royalty. That does not matter. Your husband is not the sum total of his actions. Your husband is the desire of God's heart. He is precious and honored in God's sight (Isaiah 43:4). He is made in the image of God and his value is priceless in God's eyes.

Saying yes to marriage is saying yes to being a minister of the gospel to your husband. You and I are called to be ministers of reconciliation, uniting God's creation with God, the Creator. In 2 Corinthians 5:11–21, Paul tells us to stop viewing others from a human point of view. Are you viewing your husband from a human point of view or from God's point of view? Are your thoughts about him and hopes for him consistent with God's thoughts and plans? Are your words, tone of voice, body language, and facial expressions reflecting to your husband what God says is true of him?

You have incredible influence in your husband's life. As you interact with him, you are holding up a mirror to him. You are either communicating his great value or you are telling him he is not enough.

When you look at your husband, do you focus on the areas where he seems to be lacking and the things you would like to see him improve? Or with eyes of faith, do you see that he is a human container of the Holy Spirit of the living God?

> But we have this treasure in jars of clay, to show that the surpassing power belongs to God and not to us (2 Corinthians 4:7).

As his wife, you are to walk by faith and not by sight (2 Corinthians 5:7). Your faith is a hand-in-hand walk with the God who spoke and the universe appeared. It is an "if, then" conversation with the Creator. Faith looks at God and remembers what incredible, supernatural things He has done in the past. With confidence, you realize that if the God You are relying on can do that amazing thing, then you can look forward and believe that He can do something about the current situation. Looking back at what God has accomplished is the fuel you need to look forward, believing He can do more than you can imagine.

Without faith it is impossible to please God (Hebrews 11:6). Apply that to your marriage. Without faith that God can help your husband provide for and protect you, what do you do? You react in fear. You think of all the horrible scenarios that could happen if he loses his job, can't manage the finances, embarrasses you in front of your parents, (insert your own fear here). Your thoughts become your feelings and actions toward your husband. Now the mirror you hold up to your husband has nothing to do with God's authority and power. It does not reflect God's perfect plan to prosper your husband and not to harm him (Jeremiah 29:11). It has everything to do with powerlessness, lack, and abandonment. None of those ideas honor God, who has promised to provide for all your needs because He has all the wealth of the universe.

You cannot walk away from the job of holding up the mirror to your husband. Your thoughts about him, good or bad, are obvious to him and others. And they are contagious. Think about it. What you've communicated to your parents and friends about him is the foundation where their thoughts of him originate. Are you painting a picture that looks like God's image of this man?

Looking back ten years, I realize I was so self-focused. I was blind to how my fears influenced David and those around us. I did not know how to address my concerns to David without causing a big problem. So I chose to address them with someone who would listen and take my side. In doing so, I bought myself a bigger problem. My contagious negative words built a wall between David and a few members of my family. Subsequently, walls between David and me only got thicker.

Another huge mistake I made was choosing to share my perception of the problem with people who did not have an intimate relationship with God. And so, the advice I received left God's love and power out of the equation. I did not know God as Savior of marriages then, so another divorce seemed to be on the horizon.

The shame of a second divorce lead me to a desperate "Help me, Jesus" prayer. In time, this prayer was answered. God sent His Word to me in many forms and I began to heal. The character of God became my hope. When my focus zeroed in on God, my relationship with David improved. The contagious bitterness I had once allowed to rule my life started to dry up. My thoughts and my words were beginning to agree with God's words.

Anger and fear continues to well up in me at times, but I am training myself to confess these feelings to God.

I ask God's forgiveness, and I declare that I am satisfied with God and the gifts He has given me, including my spouse. This is not a one-time event and I'm healed. It takes repetition to bring my thoughts into submission to God.

You can choose today to please God with your faith in what He has done, is doing, and has planned in your husband's mind, emotions, and body. Honor God by honoring the unique masterpiece He designed and gave to you in marriage. Take God's hand. Allow Him to lead you through this adventure of believing He is who He says He is and can do what He says He can do.

Your courageous faith in God's unlimited power will enable you to love and serve your husband as God sees him.

Prayer Prompt

Father, I look to You in awe that You created my husband, _____. You are God, the Creator of every good thing (Jeremiah 1:5; Colossians 1:16).

I am amazed that You have known him from the beginning of time. I imagine You looking at _____ and smiling. In my heart, I lean forward to see the look on Your face as you hear the sound of _____'s name. I believe that You see Your son _____, rejoice and say, he is very good! (Genesis 1:31; Zephaniah 3:17).

Your love for _____ never ends. Nothing he says or does will separate him from Your love. You paid a huge price when You sacrificed Your Son so that _____ could inherit eternal life and be adopted into Your family (1 Corinthians 13:8; Romans 5:8; Ephesians 1:5).

I confess that I am guilty of not loving _____ unconditionally. My thoughts, words, and actions do not always honor _____, Your son and incredible creation. Please forgive me for hurting You and _____ in this way. I receive Your forgiveness, Lord (1 Corinthians 13:4–7; 1 John 1:9; Romans 12:10; Isaiah 1:18; Ephesians 1:7).

Your Holy Spirit lives in me. Thank You for this gift of Your power, love, and sound mind. I invite You to open my eyes to see _____ the way You see Him. Let Your Spirit remind me of his value to You and to me (1 Corinthians 3:16; 2 Timothy 1:7; Matthew 25:40; John 14:26).

Teach me to honor him with my thoughts, my words, and my actions. Help me to see what is good and noble in him. I want to resist the temptation to focus on his weaknesses or imperfections (1 Corinthians 13:4–8; Philippians 4:8; James 4:7).

As I read Your Word, show me who _____ is because of his life in Christ (Daniel 2:22; Isaiah 55:8).

Inspire me with Your endless creativity to speak of him and to him in ways that agree with Your thoughts of him. Use me to bless him with declarations of Your truth (1 Corinthians 2:4, 13; Proverbs 18:21).

Regardless of our circumstances, I want to honor You, God, by honoring Your creation, Your son, _____.

You are where my help comes from. I relax knowing that this is Your will, and I trust that You will help me (Psalm 121:2; Isaiah 41:13).

In the name of Your perfect Son, Jesus, I pray.

Amen

A Wife's Call to Action

Choose five lines from the list of who you are in Christ in the previous chapter, and declare them over your husband. I'll get you started with two of the five.

Romans 8:1–2: My husband, David, is free from condemnation.

Ephesians 1:1: My husband, David, is a saint (consecrated, purified, and made holy).

Now choose three more and personalize them for your Mr. Forever.

Chapter 16

Honor Marriage: God's Sacred and Shared Treasure

Think for a moment about the divorces that have touched your life. Those spiritual battles against marriage have influenced you. Satan knew that you would be affected and has devised a plan to help you dishonor marriage.

My Christian, church-going parents divorced after 20 years of marriage. That summer, I found myself standing in my bedroom listening to my mom and dad walk through each room of the house deciding who got what. I knew I was in trouble. That day every conscious thought I had about marriage was labeled and filed in my brain as "wrong."

Michael, my first husband, and I married a few years after Mom and Dad separated. When we said "I do," I became his wife and a pastor's wife. I had every intention of sharing my life with him forever. Unfortunately, I had not sorted through the marriage information I had filed away.

When problems in our marriage began to emerge, I sought out Christian counseling. I poured out my tragic story to the counselor and explained to her that I could NOT get a divorce. I could not even imagine myself that way. And she said, "Jennifer, sometimes marriages die."

I also shared my fears and frustrations with my dad. I trusted him to want what was best for me and to help me. He wanted a great life for his little girl. He recommended I leave my marriage. And I did.

Why did I choose divorce? Because a few people who wore the name "Christian" and had my best interest suggested it was the right thing to do. Not once did I ask God what He thought or go to His Word with an open mind to hear from Him on the subject. There were certainly Christian friends suggesting I stay. But I chose to agree with those offering me a way out.

When problems erupted in my marriage to David, I eventually sought God. Notice I said "eventually." I made some huge mistakes before I began crying out to God for help. The gaping holes in my heart ached to be filled. My desire to be loved and seen as lovable led me down a very ugly path.

Regardless of my horrendous choices, God answered my cry for help with His Word. I began attending Beth Moore Bible studies, watching Joyce Meyer at least once a day, and found a Christian counselor who helped me apply God's Word to my life. I was so hungry for change. I pursued God for solutions. I began to honor God with my life. And my life got better! So much better.

> "Desperation is God's hammer. It demolishes the stronghold of fear and shatters the chains of our excuses. When desperation exceeds our fears, progress begins."[10]
> — Francis Frangipane

Honoring God and being obedient to His Word ultimately results in saying "yes" to His design for marriage. Hebrews 13:4 says, "Let marriage be held in honor among all, and let the marriage bed be undefiled, for God will judge the sexually immoral and adulterous." I had a choice to make. You have a choice to make. Will Jesus be the Lord and Master of your life and marriage? Will you follow Him as He leads you to honor marriage with your words and everyday life?

Honoring marriage between one man and one woman for life is counter to our culture. For every abuse, act of adultery, and divorce in this world, you will find multiple excuses as to why it was an acceptable choice. According to the culture, I made an acceptable choice when I divorced Michael. But that choice did not honor God. Leaving that marriage left even more people doubting that God had the ability to heal hearts, the strength to keep people together through the really hard conversations, and the creative power to make all things new. Satan, the master liar, was surely using my choice to his advantage.

God did heal my aching heart as His Spirit counseled me and taught me the truth of His love for me. The same God who raised Jesus from the dead carried David and me through the very difficult conversations we had been avoiding. Through the power of His Word, the Creator of the entire universe gave me a changed heart and a renewed love for David. I have experienced a total life makeover. The ashes of my original family and first marriage have been replaced with beauty. And God's not finished with me yet!

Your family dynamic and relationship skills are likely much better than mine were when I said "I do." Just remember, the enemy of your life in Christ is looking for an opportunity to chip away at your view of marriage. He had specific plans to destroy mine. And he has not overlooked your special union.

When you hear "people never change" and "you two just aren't compatible," remember my story. God changes people who choose to let Him. He is your wonderful Counselor and marriage designer. He did not fail to help me honor Him and honor marriage. He is able to do the same for you. He is able to do more than you can ask or imagine (Ephesians 3:20).

He will help you.

Prayer Prompt

Father God, You designed marriage to demonstrate your commitment to love each of us faithfully and forever. Thank you for loving me and _____ perfectly, completely, and eternally (Genesis 1:27; Psalm 136:2).

I want to be honest with You and myself regarding my thoughts about marriage. I've seen so many divorces and betrayals, including _____ (name the ones that affected you very personally). I have failed to honor marriage in the past. Please forgive me for these specific ways I've failed to honor marriage as You created it: _____ (Proverbs 28:13; Hebrews 13:4).

Because of these experiences, I am not sure I understand marriage as You created it to be. Grant me a true picture of marriage according to Your design (James 1:5; Proverbs 2:6).

Help me to experience Your love and commitment to me. With a heart filled by Your amazing love, I will be able to give steadfast love and honor to _____ (Ephesians 3:18–19; 1 John 4:19; 2 Timothy 1:7).

Let Your Holy Spirit open my eyes to Your wisdom on how to be the wife of _____. Show me in Your Word and teach me through Your appointed people what I have committed to in my marriage to _____. Let the power of Your truth overcome the lies I have learned and believed so that I live in agreement with Your will. Convict me daily so that I can repent and strengthen my commitment to You and _____ (James 1:5; John 14:26).

I need Your help to guard my heart against bitterness, selfishness, and temptation to pursue the attention of other men. Be my gentle shepherd. Lead me away from the activities and relationships that would keep me from prioritizing our marriage over every other earthly relationship (Philippians 2:3; Matthew 6:13; Psalm 23:1; Hebrews 13:4).

I rely on Your victorious power over sin to help us keep our marriage bed pure. I worship You by submitting to Your Word and honoring Your plan for marriage. In obedience to You, I give my body, the temple of your Holy Spirit, as a living sacrifice. I joyfully give my body to my husband _____ (1 Corinthians 6:18; Romans 12:1).

I invite You to bring mature Christian couples into our lives to model submission, love, and intimacy as taught in Your perfect Word. Direct us away from the influence of those who do not honor Your design for marriage (Titus 2; Psalm 32:8; Proverbs 3:5–6).

Let Your light shine in me as a gift of love to _____. As we humble ourselves at Your feet, let our marriage point to You as the perfect love (Matthew 5:14–16; 1 Peter 5:6; James 4:10; Ephesians 5:21–33).

With Jesus Christ, Your Son, as my intercessor, I pray these things.

Amen

ᘰ A Wife's Call to Action ᘰ

Find at least one Christian woman who has been married over 30 years and invite her to share with you how she has chosen to honor marriage. If you struggle to find someone, ask God to highlight one for you. He will do it!

Here are a few questions you might ask her:

- Has being married always been easy?

- How did you choose to stay married during the difficult times?

- What temptations did you experience?

- Did you have to give up anything to honor your marriage?

- What benefits are you experiencing because you have honored your marriage so many years?

Chapter 17

Honor Your Spouse: God's Sacred and Shared Treasure

Along with honoring our marriages, God instructs us to honor (respect) our husbands.

> And let the wife see that she respects her husband (Ephesians 5:33).

When I married David, I fully intended to be a great wife. There was only one problem. I didn't know how. As I mentioned before, I did not understand the meaning of honor when I married. I knew how to cook what he liked. It was natural to create a home where his kids had fun and felt at home. I knew to rub his feet and back to make him feel special. But I did not know how to trust him with my thoughts, feelings, and insecurities.

What does being a "great wife" mean to you? Where are your "great wife" character traits rooted?

My insecurities and unspoken feelings boiled under the surface of my smiles. They spilled over as I talked about him to my friends and my parents. I had no idea how much damage I was doing to our relationship. My words and my tone were as destructive as hurricane winds blasting away at the foundation of our marriage.

On the inside, I bristled to David's touch like a porcupine. Outwardly, anxiety and fibromyalgia stood between us. But one week God intervened. That Tuesday, our pastor and David's men's small group leader taught the men of the church how the Bible instructs us to handle conflict in marriage. I can still see the street I was on when David called my cell phone to tell me what he had learned. I remember feeling and seeing hope that day.

Later that week, we attended a Gary Smalley marriage seminar at our church. Dr. Smalley taught us many things that weekend. The one major takeaway for both of us was to honor your spouse with your words and actions. (If you haven't studied honor yet, I highly recommend Gary Smalley's resources. I've listed them for you in the appendix and at prayersfornewbrides.com.)

In the seminar, God opened my eyes to the personality traits that He gave to David. In a fun and gentle way, God painted a picture of the David that He had fearfully and wonderfully made. I had been guilty of looking at things about David as wrong and needing to be changed. But God made him to think that way. I had not only dishonored David, but also the amazing God who created him.

We committed to honoring each other. David was great at it. I had to work hard at breaking old habits. Our conversations with each other changed. God was faithful to open our eyes to see good things in the other person. He used other people who liked David to help me see past my own grumbling spirit. Thanks to the good words I heard myself and others say, my brain had good emotions associated with the man I lived with.

The marriage of the Bible began to be the marriage I was living. Honoring God and David, His creation, replaced the failing foundation my words worked to destroy. My very real fear that David might reject me melted away. The scary shadows of being unlovable that had once danced in my head vanished over time.

The following prayer will help you talk to God on this subject. In praying it, you will be agreeing with what God wants for your marriage. God has promised that when you pray according to His will, He will certainly answer those prayers.

Prayer Prompt

Father, Your kingdom is a place of honor. Your Word teaches me to honor Your Word and Your name above all things. I want to obey and live a life that honors You (1 Corinthians 10:31; 1 Samuel 2:30).

You know better than I do how my sinful nature wrestles with honoring You and others. Please convict me in this area. Show me my sin. I confess to You that I struggle to honor You, Your Word, and my husband, _____, in these ways _____
____ (Hebrews 2:9; Psalm 69:5, 138:2; Isaiah 29:13).

Make me ready to be used as a vessel of honor in my marriage to _____. Teach me to honor You. Highlight for me good and bad examples of honor so that I learn the difference between the two. Teach me not to tear down my husband, Your creation, with my words. Save me from becoming a quarrelsome and fretful wife that causes _____ to want to live alone (1 Corinthians 10:31; 2 Timothy 2:21; Ephesians 1:17; Proverbs 14:1, 18:21, 21:19).

Pursue me relentlessly on this until my nature is to esteem him with my every thought and word. I submit my mind to Your authority and take every disrespectful thought about _____ captive in obedience to You (Ephesians 5:33; Romans 12:2; 2 Corinthians 10:5).

Let Your Spirit living in me guide me to communicate with _____ without nagging, manipulating, belittling, or deceiving him. I want him to be able to trust me. I will need new skills for this. Please connect me to the people and resources that will teach me and mentor me in this way (Proverbs 21:19, 31:10–12; Galatians 5:22; Titus 2:4–5).

You also desire that I honor _____ by submitting to his authority. I trust You and submit to You in this way. I know You will reward me for my obedience to You (Colossians 3:18; 1 Peter 3:5; James 4:7; Romans 8:7; Ephesians 5:21; John 14:23; Isaiah 1:19).

The enemy of Your plan for my marriage has been defeated by Jesus' work on the Cross. Our marriage can and will overcome every evil snare by Jesus' blood and the words of my testimony. With Your power, love, and sound mind living in me, I will honor my husband, _____ (1 Corinthians 15:57; Revelation 12:11; 2 Timothy 1:7).

With Jesus, I pray these words as an offering to You.

Amen

A Wife's Call to Action

In his book *Fun Loving You*, Ted Cunningham recommends creating a "Fun Loving You" list. On it, you write a lengthy list why your spouse is fun to love. I can think of no better way for you and me to practice honoring our husbands.

Keep this list in an easy-to-find place so that you can add to it often. This is now your "go-to" list on those days you get hit with the thought, "Why did I marry this guy!" I know that sounds ridiculous today. But it is a very real and not so unique tactic that the enemy will use to chip away at your decision to faithfully endure the poorer days, the sickness days, and the you-make-me-want-to-scream days.

Just as you fortify your mind for your next trip to the grocery store or mall, you can fortify your marriage by keeping the "Fun Loving You" list.

Chapter 18

Sacrifice Your Expectations

What do you expect marriage to do for you? I challenge you to really pursue the answer to that question. Perhaps you've been dreaming of the beautiful wedding since you were small. Maybe your imaginings moved past the wedding to a home with a specific feel to it with a certain number of children. Did you decide marriage would be great if your husband were just like your sweet daddy? Or maybe you don't want him to be anything like the father-figure in your life. I'm confident you've got some expectations attached to being married and the man you've married. God knows them all.

Somewhere deeper than my conscious thoughts, I thought marriage would be proof that I was valuable and lovable. Some of you are sighing right now for me, aren't you? Yeah, it was a recipe for disaster.

Hindsight is 20/20, or so they say. Now, I can look back at not one but two marriages and know that I was looking for the "lovable" stamp of approval. My husband was under pressure to like everything about me, and I was VERY busy trying to be completely lovable so he would want to marry me. Can you hear the tornado sirens? Disaster, I tell you.

Of course, I wanted him to be kind, gentle, and generous like my dad. Because to me, Dad equaled what every man should be.

I had no idea at the time how complex the dad factor could be in choosing a mate. Maybe you worked that all out in advance of saying "I do." But I didn't.

Without realizing it, I was busy evaluating his reaction to my every move. Why? I wanted him to see me as "lovable." And if he looked like he was going to disapprove, I was going to do something different or be someone different. I had no idea how to be me. I was striving to be "the one" he could love.

Okay, wait. You might be ready to put this book down because the author has more issues than this book has pages. But hang on. I'm living proof that God can bring beauty from a tall pile of ashes, or in this case — expectations. If God can free me from demanding expectations, He can surely help you with yours.

With every failed expectation, I grew very disgruntled with David. I started to convince myself that I had made another bad choice for a spouse. Because David wasn't kind, gentle, and generous to me in the same ways my dad had been, I disapproved. With each disapproving thought, my heart pulled further away from David.

It didn't take long for me to drop the lovable ball in David's eyes. I did not meet several of his expectations. For me, that was the worst. In my mind, if I couldn't please him in every way, then I had failed at being the "lovable Jennifer White." Failure was not an option for me. But I couldn't repair the gap between the real Jennifer and the "perfect spouse" expectations I had of myself. So to save face, I was angry and distant. But David didn't know I was angry. I didn't bother to tell him. I just told all my girlfriends and, occasionally, my parents.

I had no idea how to handle conflict so I just avoided it. I played the role of wife and searched for a solution to my lovable issues. When our relationship problems finally erupted, I had to face the music. I had way too much pride to be divorced a second time. Several times a day, I literally cried out to God, "Please help me!" And He did.

In the Gary Smalley seminar I mentioned earlier, God helped me see the differences in David's personality and mine. When Dr.

Smalley invited those whose personality was the same as David's to stand up, approximately one-fourth of the room stood with him. All this time, I had been judging David's differences as "wrong." But he was not wrong. He was just different than me. And he was different from my dad, too.

God used that one simple exercise to change my point of view. I began to look at the Creator of David in awe of His creativity. God was suddenly so much bigger. David didn't have to fit in the box I had for him, because the ONE who designed Him for this life and this marriage had bigger plans than I had ever imagined.

I have given you just one glimpse of how God helped me to release my expectations of David and marriage. He has been my wonderful Counselor. Through His perfect Word, He has helped me learn to trust Him to meet my needs. The more I've grown to trust God, the more satisfying our marriage has become. Since marriage was His idea, I can count on Him to lead me on this adventure of letting His love empower me to faithfully love my husband.

Imagine your expectations are hanging in the grand closet of your heart. This is the closet where your spiritual armor is also stored. As your armor, through your relationship with God, takes up more space in your heart, there will be less room for or need of the expectations. With a willing and open heart toward God, you can release your "marriage must be THIS way" expectations. The extra room in your heart will be a relief and make way for the beautiful marriage God has in store for you.

Prayer Prompt

I worship You, God, the Creator of covenant marriage between one man and one woman. Without You, no one would know lasting love or the joy of a faithful marriage. Your love is better than life. You've given us marriage so that we grow in our understanding of how faithfully and mercifully You love us (Genesis 2:24; Psalm 63:3; Deuteronomy 7:9; Lamentations 3:22–23).

Thank You for the good gift of marriage to _____. I trust You have a good plan for both of us. And I choose to trust that Your plan is better than my own (James 1:17; Matthew 7:11; Jeremiah 29:11).

Only You know the list of expectations I brought to this marriage. Many people have influenced my thoughts on marriage. Media has played a big role in creating my idea of married love. I confess to You that I expected marriage to be _____. I also expected _____, my husband, to be _____. Please forgive me for limiting marriage and my husband. I have been wise in my own eyes (1 John 1:9; Proverbs 3:7).

Help me, victorious warrior, to fight against wrong thinking and motives. Holy Spirit, have Your way with my mind. I refuse to fear what I can't see in this marriage (Ephesians 1:17; Psalm 139:23; 2 Corinthians 10:5; Romans 12:2; Philippians 4:6–7; Hebrews 11:1).

I choose to set my mind on You, God. I firmly believe that nothing is impossible with You. So I open my fistful of expectations for this marriage and my husband to You. In faith, I accept the bigger unknown picture (Colossians 3:2; Luke 1:37; Hebrews 11:1).

You are the One who never needs a counselor. All wisdom comes from You! I boldly ask You for wisdom to desire from this marriage and this man what You say I should want. I am determined to follow your lead, regardless of what the world around me says I should do (Proverbs 2:6, 9:10; Romans 11:34; James 1:5).

I will seek You with all of my heart so I can know You and Your unlimited power that is available to me. Grow my faith in Your love for me and my husband. Help me to rely on You regardless of the circumstances that come against me and _____. I am safe because Your goodness and mercy pursue us daily (Jeremiah 29:13; Ephesians 3:16–19; Hebrews 11:6; Psalm 9:10, 23:6).

I release this marriage to be more than I ever imagined. Let us be known for our faithfulness to one another so that Your name will be honored. I want the stability of our relationship to cause others to desire You (Ephesians 3:20; 2 Corinthians 2:14).

I present these requests to You with great joy and confidence. I am assured that You've heard my cry for help and that I am asking in accordance with Your Word and Your will for our marriage (Matthew 7:7; Psalm 37:4, 143:1; John 14:13).

In Jesus' name.

Amen

A Wife's Call to Action

List two of your expectations of your husband (what will he do for you?).

List two of your expectations of marriage (what will marriage do for you?).

Spend some time journaling about these ideas. Ask God to reveal the root of the expectations and replace them, if needed, with His expectations.

Chapter 19

Submit to God's Leadership and Your Husband's

Submission to your husband takes enormous faith in God. Fear, pride, and a need for control all fly in the face of submitting to him. Your faith in God is your shield in the armor. It might feel heavy and almost impossible, but God's power lives within you to do what He has designed to benefit you.

David wanted to build a house for us in Branson, Missouri. Living there had been his dream for many years. We bought the land just months after we married and David started designing the house. I was all in. We were newlyweds. Of course we wanted to dream of a new adventure together!

But life together got hard. We allowed issues to go unresolved. Both of us hated confrontation. We avoided talking about the problem, and I chose to talk to everyone but him about it.

Bitterness began to embed itself in our hearts. It tainted everything. Anger brewed in my heart until I couldn't stand the thought of moving to Branson with him. I cried every time the subject came up. David would call me into his home office to show me his latest house design. My heart would sink before I got to his office. He wanted to celebrate his handiwork, and I wanted to run for the hills.

My assurance of God's faithfulness grew during a season of Bible study with the ladies of our church. I learned these five tenets of faith from the Believing God Bible study by Beth Moore:

> God is who He says He is.
> God can do what He says He can do.
> I am who God says I am.
> I can do what God says I can do.
> God's word is alive and active.[11]

Eventually I was able to trust God enough to submit to my husband's plan to build the house in Branson. I will never forget the conversation I had with God on this subject.

David is an excellent pilot and was flying us to Branson. I was sitting in the back seat of the plane reading. I was still so unsure of him, and myself, that I chose to sit in the back seat instead of the copilot's seat. The distance in my heart was more evident than I realized. We circled the city of Branson before landing. I looked out the window into the clouds and prayed: "God, I trust You. You have told me to submit to my husband. I will do that because I know You will take care of me."

That prayer of submission changed the rest of my life and our marriage. I opened my fist of fears and God laid in my hand a new life. I had not asked for this life. However, in His love for me, He planned it for me and knew it would be so much better than what I was capable of choosing on my own.

As a wife, you will have abundant opportunities to doubt your husband's leadership. Your mind and your community may encourage you to disregard his decisions. The wisdom of the world does not recommend saying yes to someone you do not trust. In fact, the world would politely call you a fool for doing so. Nevertheless, God says:

> Wives, submit [be submissive and adapt yourselves] to your own husbands as [a service] to the Lord. For the husband is head of the wife even as Christ is the head of

the church, his body, and is Himself its Savior. Now as the church submits to Christ, so also wives should submit in everything to their husbands (Ephesians 5:22–24; AMP).

God's ways are perfect. His thoughts are higher than our own thoughts and everyone else's. Your selfish nature will rebel against this biblical truth in Ephesians 5. It will cry "BUT. . . ."

But I am here to testify that I finally quit saying "BUT . . ." and said "YES" to this command. When I did, God blew my mind with blessings.

I feared moving to Branson would mean losing all my friends and being lonely. Instead I gained incredible Christian friends who opened my life to MORE community than I ever dreamed possible. I could fill ten more chapters on what I learned about God from them.

God provided a church that is focused on His design for family. We were taught by Ted Cunningham and Gary Smalley, wise preachers and counselors, from the pulpit on how to live together and love each other. David even became a part-time pilot for Gary and Ted as they traveled to lead marriage conferences at churches and Christian colleges. (Gary Smalley is a *New York Times* best-selling author on Christian marriage, and Ted Cunningham is our pastor and author of great marriage books.) David became their friend and sat under their teaching even more. I could never have asked for such a blessing.

I feared isolation. Instead I worked for our church, led Bible studies, and was given the honor of starting the church's prayer ministry.

I feared losing access to those who saw my worth. Instead, I received the blessing of working for a Christian book publisher as their vice president of marketing. I became friends with incredible authors and was given the opportunity to coach them in promoting their books. What an encouraging gift!

I could go on and on, but I want you to get busy imagining what God has waiting for you behind the "I choose to submit to my husband" door. He is faithful to bless obedience. He has been doing so since Abraham chose to obey the command to sacrifice his son Isaac.

I will surely bless you, and I will surely multiply your offspring as the stars of heaven and as the sand that is on the seashore. And your offspring shall possess the gate of his enemies, and in your offspring shall all the nations of the earth be blessed, *because you have obeyed my voice* (Genesis 22:17–18, emphasis mine).

Jesus confirmed it for us in Luke 11:28, when He responded to those honoring Mary, His mother. He said, "Blessed rather are those who hear the word of God and keep it!"

Remember James's instructions to be doers of the Word, not just hearers? He promises the reward for obedience too!

But be doers of the word, and not hearers only, deceiving yourselves. For if anyone is a hearer of the word and not a doer, he is like a man who looks intently at his natural face in a mirror. For he looks at himself and goes away and at once forgets what he was like. But the one who looks into the perfect law, the law of liberty, and perseveres, being no hearer who forgets but a doer who acts, *he will be blessed in his doing* (James 1:22–25, emphasis mine).

I'm a work in progress on this subject. Just this week, I asked a wise, godly woman to pray for me regarding a big decision I have to make. She asked me what David's advice had been and I told her. She gracefully replied:

Many times I have made the mistake of not heeding my husband's advice. It has caused tension and then eventually time has proven him correct. Then I have to apologize, repent, and move forward in the direction he advised. I am getting increasingly better at following his leadership even when it makes me uncomfortable.

As I submit to his leadership in decisions like this, he feels admired, trusted, respected. I feel safer as I am under his covering. And the increased unity is so good.

Relief washed over me as I read her words. I knew God was delivering the answer I asked Him for.

It thrills my soul to tell you that I know God is faithful to shepherd you as you obey Him. He designed the path you are meant to take. He will not get distracted or lost as He leads you. He is able to use what appears to be very wrong to bring something mind-blowing and so right!

Let Him lead you in obeying Him and submitting to your husband. You will NOT be disappointed.

Prayer Prompt

God, I thank You for having a great plan for my life and my marriage. I know that You have been patient with me as I learn to trust Your leadership and Your Word (Jeremiah 29:11; Psalm 103:8).

Grant to me the courage I need to surrender my will. I want my strength to be in following Your lead. Regardless of fearful thoughts, I want to honor You by submitting to _____ (Psalm 27:14; Joshua 1:9; Ephesians 5:22).

Jesus, You are my example of obedience to God. With complete confidence in God, You choose to live for Him and not in competition with Him. I do not want one moment of my life to compete with God's authority. Guide me to make faith-filled decisions to follow my husband's leading (1 Peter 2:22; Romans 12:2).

Holy Spirit, be my reminder of this command of submission to God and _____. Fill my mind with examples of others who have lived this way. Encourage me to look forward to the reward God has promised to bring (John 14:26; 1 Corinthians 2:9).

I choose to live as a victorious bride of Christ and
_____. My community will know me as a godly wife
and be inspired to trust You even more. By Your grace and
power, my light will shine brightly, leading others to honor
Your Word (John 3:29; Matthew 5:16).

To You, God, be all the honor.

Amen

A Wife's Call to Action

Evaluate your willingness to submit to your husband. On a scale of
1 to 10 (10 being completely surrendered) how well do you think
you are doing, or will do, on this?

You can begin moving that number higher by memorizing
Ephesians 5:22–24 and journaling about it.

Invite God to show you areas where submission will be needed
and ask Him to prepare you.

Chapter 20

Give Your Love Selflessly

Does your giving have a breaking point? The enemy of your marriage will test it. Get ready!

On a drive to Branson, I released my frustration to God. Why did He design men and women to communicate so differently? How could He expect us to get along, to stay together when we think so differently? Was this a cruel joke? Marriage is too hard! How are we supposed to do this?

God answered my question as I continued to drive. He gently reminded me that love gives. It was one of the most important conversations God and I have had about marriage.

I had been thinking about receiving the entire time. It was a selfish frame of mind. At the most, I was willing to meet David halfway in giving intimate touches, mercy for mistakes, and permission to be unique. It was a natural response in a marriage relationship, but it wasn't a godly response.

I shared with you about finally waking up to the reality that 1 Corinthians 13 love was the way God loved me. God was answering the prayer I had prayed for so long: "Lord, show me who You truly are, and who I am to You." It was the beginning of a new Jennifer White: a Jennifer who could finally receive God's love. Receiving God's love for me freed me to give love. I stopped being so needy and started being able to give love without strings attached or anger in my heart.

There were still areas of woundedness in my heart that made giving to David seem impossible. My fears and insecurities regarding sexual intimacy made giving love to David in this important way a major challenge. I learned to invite God to love David through me. If God's strength could be made perfect in my weakness, then I could give Him this weakness of mine and let Him be strong. He does. The God who loves my husband perfectly and knows his every need, uses my body as vessel to deliver love to David. My choice to give love to David is an act of worshiping God.

Your challenges to give love could be very different than mine. Your woundedness or selfishness may surface in other areas of your marriage. Regardless of the effect, the underlying cause could be your ability to receive love from God.

We love because he first loved us (1 John 4:19). The more I learn who God is, the more I recognize His loving acts toward me. And my anxieties and heartaches decrease! This will be true for you as well. There is no problem in you, your spouse, or your marriage that God cannot resolve. Nothing that comes against your marriage is stronger than God.

Prayer Prompt

I bow my knee to You, the Creator of marriage. You graciously offer me and _____ the gift of Your perfect love. Please help us both to grasp this truth about You. You know the gaping holes in my heart, the lies I've believed about You and what You think about me. Let Your Holy Spirit place the salve of Your true love on these places within my mind and heart and marriage (Philippians 2:10–11; Romans 5;5, 8; John 8:32; Romans 5:5; Psalm 103:3).

At Your feet, I lay my desire to love _____ the way You have ordained me, as his wife, to love him. I am weak, but You are strong. I surrender my heart, body, and mind to the obedience of Christ and choose to imitate the selfless love Christ has shown me (Matthew 15:30; 2 Corinthians 10:5, 12:9–10; Ephesians 5:1–2).

I confess to You the selfish ways I have interacted with _____. Bring to my mind my selfish ways that I do not see so that I can confess them to You (1 John 1:9; John 14:26).

I admit that I am weak in the areas of loving _____ in these ways: _____, _____, _____, and _____ (2 Corinthians 10:9).

But Your Spirit lives in me. It is the same Spirit that raised Jesus from the dead. If you can resurrect a man who has been dead for three days, you can certainly resurrect the dead places in my heart, my husband's heart, and this marriage (Romans 8:11).

Jesus, be my gentle Shepherd. Corral me so that I am consistently in Your Word and influenced by others who obey You. I want to love You by obeying Your commands (Psalm 23:1; John 14:21, 16:13; Joshua 1:8).

You are the author and perfecter of my faith. Help me to trust Your love and Your commands, regardless of what I experience in this marriage (Hebrews 12:2).

I want this marriage to reflect Your covenant love. Use me to that end, Lord (Colossians 3:17).

With Jesus' love abiding in me, I pray.

Amen

⌒ A Wife's Call to Action ⌒

You can give selflessly. It's God's nature to do so, and He lives in you. Choose one area in your relationship with your husband where you will intentionally give without expecting him to meet you half-way or at all.

Relax if this becomes difficult. You are human and God is using this exercise to help you see the things in yourself that the enemy will try to use against your marriage. You are proactively training yourself to be ready for the battle of your own will.

You can do this!

Chapter 21

Fear Less: Your Privilege as a Wife

One or two generations before you, women were often portrayed in books and movies as damsels in distress. They seemed weak and in need of being rescued by men. When you think of those scaredy-cat little ladies in their pearls and gloves, what rises up in your spirit? Do you roll your eyes and wish they had some backbone, or do you smile wishing you had permission to be "not so brave"?

Each of us has issues with fear. Some of us hide it well, some flaunt fear like a badge of honor, and there are some whose lives are totally hijacked by fearful thoughts. Where do you fall on the fear continuum?

In 2010 I was invited to a women's retreat. The entire event was focused on one biblical truth:

> For God gave us a spirit not of fear but of power and love and self-control (2 Timothy 1:7).

Before this retreat, I would have proudly told you that I was fearless. But with every talk, every song, and focused time of prayer, God pulled a layer of self-protective film from my heart. Looking back,

I recognize I hid my fears in an effort to appear confident and composed. But the gentle love of God's Spirit began to work the truth of 2 Timothy 1:7 into the fabric of my soul. Years later, my mind is still embracing the fact that fear is not from God.

Only God truly knows how deeply embedded fear is in your thinking. Our enemy, the tormentor, wants us to believe that our fears are permanent, immovable problems that will follow us forever. He wants them to remain hidden because he is the ruler of darkness. He rejoices when we label ourselves defective because of these fears, when in reality, he is the initiator of fear. Remember the Garden of Eden. What did Adam and Eve do when they had eaten the forbidden apple? They hid in fear.

They had sinned against God and responded in fear. After they confessed and God explained the consequences of the sin, what happened? God showed them love and mercy by replacing their fig leaves with animal skins (Genesis 3:21). Wow!

The Henry Morris Study Bible explains that God's provision of these garments teaches us that a man-made effort to prepare for God's presence will be rejected. It also shows that animals died to cover their sin. The shedding of innocent blood was required as a condition of forgiveness for the sinner. Seriously! Do you see the amazing love of this God who wants to provide His children with every opportunity to be with Him? God hates sin because it separates you from His love and His peace and the joy of His presence. He knows that an enemy wants to entrap you in a cesspool of lies and fears that will keep you focused on yourself and your circumstances and not Him. God wants his little girl to be safe in the shelter of His wing (Psalm 17:8). Jesus died so that you could know a life beyond the dark cave of fearfulness.

Old fears of rejection, abandonment, unworthiness, failure, and others will come against your sacred union. But God is ready to help you recognize the threat and move beyond it. Second Timothy 1:7 tells us that He provides love, power, and self-control.

Imagine holding up a puzzle piece that you just cannot place in the puzzle. No matter what you try, it just does not fit. In frustration, you lay it down and see three more pieces that, surprisingly, fit perfectly. That is a simple illustration of how you can recognize the fear that causes you to feel stuck, lay it down, and choose to apply God's power, love, and sound mind to your circumstances.

As a member of the Bride of Jesus Christ, you are equipped with everything you need to be a fearless bride to your husband. God supplies all of your needs. Let 2 Timothy 1:7 be the rally cry reminding you to confess your need for His power, love, and self-control. Jesus will graciously help you to operate in freedom. He is the Messiah. God sent Him to set every captive free! Helping you to live victoriously is what He was sent to do.

I sought the LORD, and he answered me and delivered me from all my fears (Psalm 34:4).

Prayer Prompt

God, Your unlimited supply of love and help amazes me. There is no one on this earth who loves me, helps me, serves me, affirms me, and provides for me like You. I am so grateful You love me with this unlimited supply (Philippians 4:19; Psalm 23:1).

You are more aware of my fearful thoughts than I am. You know why I am fearful. You are the source of healing for all of my fears. Without Your help, I will not be able to even confess my fears by name. Please hold my hand through this and help me to submit these life-draining fears under Your authority. I long to relax in Your care, knowing that You are gentle and patient with me (Psalm 18:35, 139:2; Matthew 4:23; James 4:7; 1 Corinthians 13:4).

Make fearless living a reality to me. Cause me to operate in complete knowledge of Your desire and ability to empower me to live above the veiled threats of the evil one.

I am awake to Your overcoming power (Psalm 23:1; Prov-erbs 29:25; Isaiah 41:10; Colossians. 2:15).

With Your overcoming power, I will live as a fearless wife to _____. I want to transport Your love to the deepest places of his heart. Our love will be a brilliant light, radiating the obvious truth of Your presence in our lives (John 8:12, 15:12, 16:33; 1 John 4:4, 7; Matthew 5:16).

I surrender my fears. I receive Your prolific power, love, and self-control by Your gracious hand (2 Timothy 1:7).

To You, Jesus, be the glory and honor.

Amen

A Wife's Call to Action

What fears do you see in your mom, your grandmother, and others in your family?

Have you adopted those fears as well?

They do not have to be your fears. You can evict them with the free will that God has given you. God is eager to help you identify and replace them. He can change the way you, your children, and your children's children experience life.

Memorizing and meditating on 2 Timothy 1:7 is an excellent way to begin the process of eliminating those fears from your life and marriage today. God can do more than you think in this area.

Chapter 22

Respect: Meeting Your Husband's Greatest Need

. . . and let the wife see that she respects her husband (Ephesians 5:33).

There it is. The wife's battle plan fits into one simple statement: respect your husband.

It's easy to say, but not so easy to do. It is your opportunity to love like Jesus, which includes laying down your life.

There are no conditions on the command to respect him. In fact, "see that she respects her husband" ends the section on marriage as well as the chapter. But our attitude can easily turn to something like, "Well, I would respect him if he. . . ."

You are married to an imperfect human being whose nature, at no fault of his own, is to resist God's leadership. You are not alone. Christ, our perfect Bridegroom, is also married to imperfect human beings whose nature is to resist God's leadership. You and I fail regularly to deny ourselves and follow Christ's example of obedience. Yet, Christ chose to die to His own rights for us. And now He intercedes for our needs and offers us fresh mercy for our failings each day.

Our husbands get the same renewable portion of mercy from Christ Jesus. They surely make mistakes. And God is prepared for that to happen to you. He promised you that He is your shepherd and you will not want for anything (Psalm 23:1). He is able to sustain the needs of the entire universe. Sustaining you and your marriage relationship is not too hard for Him.

It is easy to be blind to our lack of respect for our husband. God is faithful to show us where we are lacking if we humble ourselves to ask Him. In the time that I've been writing this book, I noticed myself rolling my eyes at something my husband said. I was immediately convicted. I've not always been immediately convicted! And I'm still working on treating him with my utmost respect.

Respect is defined as deference to someone with certain privileges and rights. The Bible makes it clear that your husband, no matter who he is and what he has done, has the right to your deep respect.

You are likely having a host of different emotions right now. You heart will want to respect and obey God. Your sin nature will scream "NO WAY!" You are not alone. This is hard. You will make it. I'm living proof.

I'd like to share with you two of the ways I have failed to respect my husband:

> I allowed other people's opinions to be more important than his.
>
> I shared my opinions and frustrations about his weaknesses with all the wrong people.

Today, seeing those words typed out makes my heart really sad. Back then, those behaviors were as normal to me as eating soup with a spoon. I had no idea I was sinning against God, and never bothered to think of what I was doing to David. In Genesis 2:18, God tells us that woman was created to be a helper to her husband. I was not helping. I was so blinded by my own needs. I had no idea how much I was hurting him and destroying our intimacy.

Abiding in the Word of God more than in the world is the only reason I know anything different today. Researching for this chapter and writing these words has been a wonderful refresher course for me. It has reminded me to confess to God my incredible weakness in this area. And it helps me to cry out to Him for help in living the way He knows will be the best for me.

Growing in your confidence of God's love for you will help you more than any other thing you do for yourself. As you receive 1 Corinthians 13 love from Him you will be able to give it to your husband. Until then, you will struggle with the need to compete with this man who is called by God to lead you. Trusting God to fill in the gaps for your husband's humanness (and your own) is the ticket to a joy-filled marriage where honor and respect reign.

Prayer Prompt

God, I want to trust You more. Help me to see You as the marriage designer and perfecter (Ephesians 5:22–33).

I confess to you that I am full of thoughts and opinions that do not line up with Your command. My humanness finds it very hard to respect my husband at times. Search me and reveal the root of my wrong thoughts (Psalm 139:23–24).

Slay my pride, Lord. Help me to see how imperfect I am so that I am not filled with disdain for my husband's imperfections. Let my life become one of humility and reverence of You (Proverbs 11:2; John 8:7; Philippians 2:5–11).

Let Your Holy Spirit prompt me to give 1 Corinthians 13 love to _____, regardless of our circumstances. Let Your Word renew my mind and transform my attitude toward _____. Help me to speak words to _____ and about him that will encourage him and please You. I want my love and respect for him to reflect Your love to the world. I trust that my respect for _____ will minister to him (Romans 12:1–2; 1 Thessalonians 5:11; Hebrews 10:24; Psalm 19:14; Ephesians 5:33; 1 Peter 3:1).

I rely on You for help and choose to resist the wisdom of the world. I will continually walk in Your light, confident that the blood of Jesus will cleanse me of all my sin (Matthew 6:13; 1 Corinthians 2:5; Ephesians 3:16; 1 John 1:7).

By Your grace, our marriage will draw attention to Your greatness (2 Corinthians 12:9).

With the power of the name of Jesus, I pray.

Amen

A Wife's Call to Action

Do you use a digital calendar on a smart phone? Use it to remind you of your role in your marriage to _____.

Set a daily or weekly reminder (calendar appointment) with these words as the subject: "(Your Name), see that you respect your husband today." Set it up to email you or pop up on your screen.

Partnering with God to Defend Your Husband

There is nothing that makes us love a man so much as praying for him.[12]

— William Law

Chapter 23

Praise: Your Love Song to God and First Line of Defense

How are you in the "praise" department? Are you known for seeing the best in people and encouraging them? Do you find it easy to brag on God and what He has done for you? Or do you find yourself focusing on the "issues" in people and "what if's" with God?

Praise is vital to your relationship with God. As we praise Him, we acknowledge that He is worthy of honor. We salute Him as the One who ranks higher than all people, things, and dreams. No one is worthy of being celebrated as much as God is, because God Himself gives every good gift that we enjoy (James 1:17).

When you married Mr. Right, you received a gift of indescribable value. Your husband is an original. He's God's unique expression of love, power, and creativity. There will never be another man created like the one you've married. This man is an unrepeatable miracle.

A person's value has everything to do with God, the Creator, and very little to do with individual successes and failures. God's love and favor do not hinge on a person's goodness:

The LORD is good to all, and his mercy is over all that he has made (Psalm 145:9).

For He is kind to the ungrateful and the evil (Luke 6:35).

Your husband belongs to God. If he were the only person alive, God would have allowed Jesus to leave the perfection of heaven to die just for him. God delights in your man — regardless. Regardless of his mistakes, bad manners, failed attempts to remember what is important to you, or lack of interest in your family, God celebrates him.

Will you join God in that celebration of your beloved? Will you praise God for the gift of _____?

You have committed to love, honor, and cherish God's masterpiece from now until death separates you from him. God, your gentle shepherd, will guide you and empower you to see what He sees in your husband. All you have to do is keep your eyes on God. You can praise God today because He is a faithful God and His faithfulness is applied to helping you cherish your husband.

Keep in mind that you are not the only person in this marriage fighting a spiritual battle. Your husband, who is commissioned to love you as Christ loved the Church, is most certainly a target in the sites of the deceiver. He will attempt to entice your husband to compete with God in some way. He will take advantage of opportunities to discourage your husband from relying on God for wisdom and strength to lead your family.

And what if the enemy chose to use your mouth to bring your husband down? Would he use the tactic of comparison? Would he suggest to you that your husband was less than some other man you've noticed or maybe even less capable than you? Or would he list for you every mistake your husband had made, hoping you would verbally bash your husband for all to hear?

Bashing your husband is taking a shot at God, the One who created Him.

And the King will answer them, "Truly, I say to you, as you did it to one of the least of these my brothers, you did it to me" (Matthew 25:40).

My best advice, friend, is to fill your mouth with the greatness of God so you do not have the space and time in your life to offend God in this way.

With your life focused on the greatness of God, you will enjoy His creation of your husband, regardless of the circumstances. **God will empower you to praise Him for the gift of your spouse.** He will give you courage to see in faith what He sees in this spiritual realm. He will employ your mouth to speak blessings over your husband (Proverbs 18:21).

Praise is our first line of defense in spiritual battle.

In 2 Chronicles chapter 20, we learn that King Jehoshaphat faced a battle against three armies at the same time. He recognized his need for God's intervention and called for a day of prayer and fasting. The Lord's answer was unlike any battle plan a warrior could imagine. He told them where to go, and to merely "stand firm." He explained that He was fighting for them and they would not have to do the fighting.

With faith in God's promise, Jehoshaphat arranged a choir to lead them, singing praises to God along the way to their God-given destination. The victory cheers preceded the victory. Why? Because they knew God could be trusted. This is such a beautiful example of faith in action.

How will you apply this to your marriage?

Look at the forces that threaten marriages — health, finances, addiction, communication, and more. Can you praise Him now for what He will do for you and _____? Will you let God fight the battles for you?

Can you celebrate in advance of the victory God will bring? Will you act in faith because you KNOW God will move on your behalf and accomplish more than you could dare to ask or dream?

Will you praise Him no matter what you see with your eyes and hear with your ears?

Prayer Prompt

Amazing God,

I want Jehoshaphat's faith! Grant me a deep and abiding trust in You so that I will seek Your face for wisdom and power. Fill my mind with thoughts of You. Inject my soul with the steadfast desire to praise You regardless of our circumstances (1 Corinthians 2:5; Daniel 2:20; Isaiah 26:3; 1 Thessalonians 5:18).

God, I praise You for Your amazing creative power. You created my husband, _____, with as much attention to detail as every other person in this world. You marked him with Your very own image. He is one of Your completely unique masterpieces (Genesis 1:26; Isaiah 64:8).

Your plan for him included his parents. Thank You for using his mother, _____, and father, _____, to bring _____ into the world. You knew I would be his wife before he was even born. Thank You for every influence in his life that You have used to shape his personality and his passions (Jeremiah 29:11; Ephesians 1:11).

I confess to You the times when I have desired that _____ change to be something different. I have wished that he were _____, _____, and _____ (1 John 1:9).

Purify my mind, Lord. Transform my thoughts by the power of Your Word. Show me where and when my thoughts about _____ do not agree with Your thoughts. Ignite in me an unquenchable desire to see him as You see him. Let Your Holy Spirit be my husband-appreciating coach, pointing out to me his noble and praiseworthy attributes (2 Corinthians 7:1; Romans 12:2; John 14:26; Philippians 4:8).

Thank you for the influence You have given me in
_____'s life. Use me to affirm him, his purpose in
Your kingdom, and the gifts You have given him. When he
looks into my eyes, I want him to experience Your love and
compassion. When he hears my voice calling his name, let
him hear Your voice delighting in him. When he hears me
talk about him, confirm for him the value of his life as Your
creation (1 Peter 3:1; Ephesians 5:1, 33; Zephaniah 3:17).

Your plans for _____ are good. The gifts You have
given him are many. I celebrate the gifts of _____,
_____, _____, and _____ you've
woven into him. Thank You, Lord, for Your unlimited
wealth of resources, wisdom, and strength available to
_____. With Your gifts, Your leadership, and Your
power, _____ will fulfill the purposes You brought
him to life to accomplish (Jeremiah 29:11; Romans 12:6–
8; 1 Peter 4:10; Psalm 50:10; Ecclesiastes 5:19; James 1:5;
Ephesians 2:10, 3:16).

Thank You for making me one with this man, Your
unique work of art (Matthew 19:5–6; Ephesians 2:10).

A Wife's Call to Action

Review the following verses and use them to write your own prayer
to God.

One thing have I asked of the LORD, that will I seek
after: that I may dwell in the house of the LORD all the
days of my life, to gaze upon the beauty of the LORD and to
inquire in his temple (Psalm 27:4).

Death and life are in the power of the tongue, and
those who love it will eat its fruits (Proverbs 18:21).

Honor everyone . . . (1 Peter 2:17).

Love one another with brotherly affection. Outdo one another in showing honor (Romans 12:10).

Whoever oppresses a poor man insults his Maker, but he who is generous to the needy honors him (Proverbs 14:31).

Whatever is true, whatever is honorable, whatever is just, whatever is pure, whatever is lovely, whatever is commendable, if there is any excellence, if there is anything worthy of praise, think about these things (Philippians 4:8).

Let everything that has breath praise the LORD! (Psalm 150:6).

Chapter 24

Nurture His Soul Through Intercession

God has given you to your husband as a helpmate (Genesis 2:18). As his wife, you have great influence in more areas than you've ever imagined. His relationship with God is the most important one.

Your influence, however, does not give you license to "attempt" to control his relationship with God. There will be days when you would like to be in control of your spouse's interactions with God. You might want him to read his Bible more, pray more, confess certain sins, and serve God more often with his time. You will be tempted to blame issues in your marriage on his lack of participation in one or more of those activities.

When I began reading the *The Power of a Praying Wife* by Stormie Omartian, I felt powerful. I was helping my husband in the best way I could imagine. I was praying for him. Everything about the process felt right to me. As I finished the first prayer, I choked on the final sentence, "Lord, give my husband a new wife, and let it be me."[13] What? A new wife? Wait, Stormie is suggesting that as a wife, I need to change? Hang on a minute. I'm praying for David here, not me.

But I knew deep in my soul those words were very true. I needed to get the plank out of my own eye before I thought another minute about the splinter sticking out of David's (Matthew 7:5).

Like me and every other wife, you will be very tempted to focus on how he needs to change. Your pride will work overtime to make his faults seem worse than yours. And the more you think and talk about his faults, the bigger and more ghastly they become in your mind.

Interceding for your husband needs to flow from a heart full of tender mercy. You cannot give mercy to him, unless you have needed it first. Facing your own sin, your weaknesses, and brokenness will make you a better wife.

The level of intimacy and close proximity a couple experiences in marriage only helps to make sin more evident. In *Sacred Marriage*, author Gary Thomas explains, "I wouldn't be surprised if many marriages end in divorce largely because one or both partners are running from their own revealed weaknesses as much as they are running from something they can't tolerate in their spouse."[14] God loves you and your husband regardless of those little or big things that make you want to point, maybe even shake, your finger.

You both wake up to fresh mercy from God each day (Lamentations 3:22–23).

When you've had the plank in your eye surgically removed in God's operating room (time in His Word and at His feet in prayer), you will look at the splinter in your husband's eye and feel compassion. You will know the pain of having it removed and the relief of living without it. Then you will empathize with the fear, insecurity, or pain that hides behind his behavior.

You can rely on God's Spirit in you to demonstrate His love, joy, peace, patience, kindness, faithfulness, gentleness, and self-control (Galatians 5:22–23). Ultimately, your husband will feel more loved and less threatened by you and your expectations. He will see you as his helper and trust you more with his struggles and weaknesses.

Interceding for your husband and modeling a deep love for God are priceless gifts you can always give. Talking about his relationship with God is something you can ask the Holy Spirit to initiate. Communicating with your husband about intimate subjects can be easy for you and difficult for other wives in your neighborhood. Every marriage is unique, and God knows the personalities, experiences, and circumstances involved in yours. With the same power that raised Jesus from the dead, God can bring your husband close to Himself. He is able to make all things work together for good for you and your husband (Romans 8:28).

I want to caution you not to assume the role of Holy Spirit to your husband. God knows every need in your husband and in your marriage. He is able to bring wisdom, correction, and comfort to your husband without one word from you (1 Peter 3:1). Ask God to minister His great love to your husband. Seek God on his behalf, reaching up to the endless supply of heaven for him. Knock, and God will open the doors of heaven on your husband's behalf (Matthew 7:7).

In *The Circle Maker: Praying Circles around Your Biggest Dreams and Greatest Fears*, Mark Batterson explains, "Prayers are prophecies. They are the best predictors of your spiritual future. Who you become is determined by how you pray. Ultimately, the transcript of your prayers becomes the script of your life."[15] So, apply that to your marriage. Your prayers for yourself and your husband determine the course of your marriage. The following prayer will guide you in being a helpmate to your husband as an intercessor.

Prayer Prompt

Father, I am thrilled to be _____'s wife and it is a privilege to serve him as an intercessor. I am grateful that Jesus sits at Your right hand and intercedes for _____ day and night. Jesus' Spirit in _____ hears the cries of his heart that I'm not even aware of, and intercedes. What a gift! I am relieved that I do not carry the weight of this responsibility alone. I want to partner with Jesus, as I intercede. My heart and mind are tuned to You, ready to receive Your promptings to pray for _____ in the specific ways only You know he needs (Romans 8:26, 34; Matthew 11:29–30).

Thank You for the intensity of Your love for my man. You created him for the purpose of being in relationship with You. I want to do my part in encouraging this by the example of my own relationship with You. Compel me to live out my relationship with You so that _____ is inspired. Help me to ignore every fear and distracting thought that seeks to hide my witness to _____ in this way (Genesis 1:26–2:3; 1 Peter 3:1–4; 2 Corinthians 10:5).

I admit that I sometimes struggle to recognize _____'s relationship with You. This causes me to judge _____ as if he is not doing his part in connecting with You. I confess this sin of judgment and ask You to forgive me. Help me to replace any judgments with loving intercession (Matthew 7:1).

I know men often relate and communicate differently than women. So I release to You my expectations for _____'s relationship with You to look and sound a certain way. Grant me the gift of Your perspective, Lord. Give to me the courage I need to communicate with _____ openly about his relationship with You. Let my heart toward him on this subject be pure. Go before us in these conversations, and break down in both of us any walls of fear and pride that exist (Romans 11:34; Ephesians 1:16–19; Joshua 1:9; Psalm 51:10; Deuteronomy 31:8; Proverbs 29:23).

My heart's cry for _____ is that he would know You, the God of the Bible, and know who he is to You. Tear down any misconceptions that he has about You. Help him to see that You are the God that gives 1 Corinthians 13 love: patient, kind, and enduring love to him. I invite You to teach him Your character and roles in his life. Help him to know You as his defender, his counselor, his shepherd, his comforter, his encourager, his Savior, and so much more (Isaiah 6, 9:6; Psalm 18:1, 23:1; John 14:1, 15:26; Luke 1:47).

With Your guidance, _____ will grow in his desire to seek You and study Your Word. My hope is that You would send him many male influences that would model this life in Your Word. As he studies and applies Your truths, he will be competent and equipped for every good work You've created for him to complete with Your help (Psalm 48:14, 119:11, 18; 2 Timothy 3:14–17).

Only Your Word can cleanse and purify _____. I invite You to wash him in the water of Your Word. Let _____ be a man willing to confess his sins to You, with confidence that You are faithful to forgive him. I praise You for the new mercy You have waiting for _____ every single day of his life (Ephesians 5:26; 1 John 1:9; Lamentations 3:22–23).

Inspire _____ to live in obedience to Your Word. Remind him of the peaceful and confident life You deliver when he lives out Your instructions. I want his heart and mind to be brimming with joy and peace. Because of his relationship with You, his life will be hope-filled! (James 1:22–25; Isaiah 32:17; Luke 11:22; Romans 15:13).

You created _____ to reflect Your strength and confidence. Oh, that Your Holy Spirit would shield _____'s eyes from the world's self-sufficient idea of manhood. Nurture in _____ a willingness to surrender his will and run this race to accomplish Yours (Psalm 37:7; Acts 5:39; 1 John 2:16–17; Hebrews 12:1).

God, You know far better than either of us what _____ needs to live for You. I praise You, _____'s true leader. I trust You are leading him in ways I've never imagined. I see with eyes of faith that You are leading him to victory. Use _____ to spread the knowledge of Your love like a sweet aroma to me and all who come in contact with him (Isaiah 55:8; Romans 8:14; 2 Chronicles 13:12; Psalm 23:2; 1 Corinthians 15:57; 2 Corinthians 2:14).

My desire is that every aspect of _____'s life be used to make Your name famous (1 Corinthians 10:21).

In Jesus' name, I pray these things.

Amen

A Wife's Call to Action

Take some time to pray or journal with God on this quote:

God never gives us discernment in order that we may criticize, but that we may intercede.[16] — Oswald Chambers

Chapter 25

Saluting His Spiritual Authority with Eyes of Faith

What are your expectations of your husband in the area of spiritual leadership? Have the two of you talked about your desire to be led by him in spiritual matters as well as all others? It's likely that you have married a strong spiritual leader who will spend the rest of your marriage blowing your mind by his devotion to God and his family. On the off chance that this is not your experience, I am going to address it.

Many Christian wives have complained that their husbands do not lead in this way. I have been one of those wives. Satan delights to whisper dissatisfaction to a wife about her husband's relationship to God in hopes of driving a wedge between them. Imagine his victory dance if you would resent your husband because of a *perceived* lack of relationship with God. So, before you become a wife who is disappointed in this area, I want you to consider this. . . .

This is a problem that started with Adam and Eve and not in your marriage. Now, we have to face the fact that Eve, the woman, set the stage for this failure with her choice not to run a major spiritual decision by her husband. Ouch! When Eve and then Adam disobeyed God, they put into motion a relationship problem we are still addressing. Wives struggle to allow their husbands to lead, and husbands struggle to take the role of leader.

Eve was the first controlling, overbearing wife. Let's acknowledge that her choice to lead was outside the will of God. It opened the door to a host of marital devastations that God did not intend for any of us.

Eve acted out of fear that she was missing out on the best. This scheme worked on Eve, and be warned: our enemy continues to employ it today. You will be tempted to jump ahead of your husband. You will want something that you believe is best for your marriage. And you will be tempted to believe he will not make the right decision. You *might* even find yourself thinking, "If he won't be obedient to God, I must make sure we are." Because you are there to *help* him get it right. Right?

One day you may hear your human nature scream something like this:

> "NO WAY. I have to protect myself from his potentially bad decisions."
>
> "We may never get to where God is leading us if I let him lead."
>
> "What if he makes the wrong decision, then what?"
>
> "He's not in the Word enough. He misses church for _____. How will he know what God wants him to do?"
>
> "He looks like a perfect husband and devoted Christian at church, but when we get home I see the real deal."

As wives, we are wired to desire protection and security. Our deepest need is to feel safe and secure in our marriage. This need in us tends to welcome fear as if it is necessary to survive.

Our true security is found in God, the One who sent us a Savior. Jesus died to rescue us from ourselves and grant us the freedom to live in unity with God. Our unity with God is a gift we receive when we trust He is our answer. We MUST follow the instructions of the One saving us or risk being captured, and held captive by our enemy.

Here are our instructions:

> Likewise, wives, be subject to your own husbands, so that even if some do not obey the word, they may be won without a word by the conduct of their wives, when they see your respectful and pure conduct (1 Peter 3:1–2).

We are to subject ourselves to our husbands, even if they are not obeying the Word. Why? Because God designed the man, knows his every thought and motive, and knows how he will come to a life surrendered to Jesus. It is God's design that your respect for your husband and your obedience to God will cause your husband to desire God.

Imagine a rescue scene in a movie where the hero tells the captive to do A, B, and C. Then, in fear, the captive just stares at the hero saying, "No, I can't, I'm scared." Meanwhile, the enemy is getting closer and closer. God, the hero in our story, is telling us what to do and how to avoid the pitfalls He knows the enemy has planned.

God tells us what to do to enjoy the love relationship He designed. We have a choice. Follow Him to safety or wait in fear, allowing our choices to play a strong role in sabotaging our marriage.

Please! Do not do what I have done. Do not let your fear convince you to lead your family. Trust God to be the hero of your story.

Remember who God is and what He has done. Protecting you and simultaneously growing your husband as the spiritual leader is not too hard for Him.

Salute your husband's spiritual authority by giving God the "Yes, Sir" on this one. With eyes on God we can celebrate the victory we see or trust that God is bringing. And we exhale in relief that God is fighting for us, defending us, protecting us, and working in ways that our minds cannot comprehend.

You are designed to be your husband's helper (Genesis 2:18). Help him by praying. Help him by doing everything you do as unto

God. Let him experience your devotion, your adoration, your trust in God. He may make fun of you for it. And that will be tough to take. Jesus was mocked and it did not deter Him. He lives in you, offering you His strength to endure it and continue to offer love to your man.

If your husband is leading your family into known sin and illegal activity, pray for help! Ask God to bring the truth to the light, to give you boldness and favor with your husband. Invite God, your supplier, to give you wisdom on when to speak, who to speak to, and what to do next.

Prayer Prompt

Almighty God, You are my shield and defender. Thank You! With Your power and love, You shelter me from evil (Psalm 91:1–2, 54:4–7).

You have given me to _____ as his helpmate. Thank You for this gift of purpose (Genesis 2:18; Ephesians 2:10).

You are able to keep me safe while You help _____ to lead me. Thank You. Help me to grow in faith in this fact. I want to act obediently even when I cannot anticipate what You will do. Give me the faith of Moses who obeyed Your command to raise his staff over the Red Sea. You parted a sea and made a way for the Israelites to escape doom. I trust You to do the same for us (2 Thessalonians 3:3; Hebrews 12:2; Romans 6:16; Exodus 15).

Forgive me for the many ways I have discouraged _____'s spiritual leadership. I confess my disregard of Your leadership, Lord. I am guilty of ignoring Your instructions. I forgive _____ for his failings and admit that I have actually helped him fail by taking control in decision-making. Be merciful to us both, Lord (Matthew 6:12–15; Ephesians 2:3–5; Psalm 41:4).

Fill me with faith that praises You and my husband for leading me (Ephesians 2:8–9; Hebrews 13:15).

Use me to encourage _____ as the leader in our home. Fill my mind and my mouth with words that affirm him. Help me to daily demonstrate my confidence in him (1 Thessalonians 5:11; Psalm 19:14).

Grant to us the fearless courage and leadership of Joshua and Caleb who saw an impossible situation and boldly acknowledged Your power and faithfulness to achieve victory. Give us the spiritual vision of Paul to trust You and live in full devotion to You and obedience to Your Word (Numbers 13–14; Acts 9:18).

Appoint to _____ the teachers and mentors who will help him to forsake the wisdom of this world and cling to Your Word for direction. Bring into my life the same Lord. Purify our hearts. Renew our minds. Help us to be sheep that hear Your voice and follow You, our Good Shepherd (Titus 2; Psalm 51; John 10:1–21).

I will remain confident that You began a good work in me and _____ and You are actively completing it, making us into Your own image (Philippians 1:6; 2 Corinthians 5:17).

I choose today to serve You in obedience by allowing _____ to lead. I will pursue Your kingdom rules and trust that my needs will never go unmet. You promised and I believe that "all these things will be added to me." I believe that includes _____'s spiritual leadership in our marriage (Joshua 24:15; Ephesians 5:22–35; Matthew 6:33; Psalm 23:1; Philippians 4:19).

My lips will never stop praising You. You are faithful! (Psalm 63:3; 2 Thessalonians 3:3).

In Jesus' faithful name I pray.

Amen

A Wife's Call to Action

Is your husband already leading you with his devotion to Jesus as Lord? Take some time to praise God and your husband for that beautiful gift you are experiencing.

Are you already wrestling with the desire for your husband to lead you in prayer, in making decisions that honor God and His Word? I want to encourage you to do these three things:

1. Talk to God about it. Tattle on your husband to God. Share your disappointments with God and ask God to minister to you there. Let Him fill your heart with His love and tender care for you. Ask Him to encourage you and give you moment-by-moment wisdom on how to handle it His way.

2. Look for the people and resources God will put in your path to help you navigate this issue. Many other women are wrestling with this. Many other women are living on the other side of the struggle. Ask them how to handle the specific situations you are facing.

3. Exercise your faith in God's ability to do more than you can ask or imagine in you, as an example, and in your husband. Start a list of all the things you believe God can do to help you and your husband. Add to the list often. As your faith in God grows, so will this list.

Chapter 26

Reinforcing His Role as Provider and Protector

He is your knight in shining armor. That's what you've imagined, right? He's going to rescue you. Do we blame Disney for this dream with roots deep in our hearts? Maybe not.

God sent Jesus to save you. You were designed to look for a Savior.

> For the husband is the head of the wife even as Christ is the head of the church, his body, and is himself its Savior (Ephesians 5:23).

> Husbands, love your wives, as Christ loved the church and gave himself up for her (Ephesians 5:25).

As a wife, your heart longs to know that he will guard your body and defend your home. You long to live free from the worry of short supply. You want it to be safe to need him.

Your expectations of his role as your protector and provider are good. He was created to do exactly that. He is assigned to do it. His leadership role in your life is critical to the success of your marriage.

Remember that we live in a world where sin abounds and the media paints life way outside the lines the Bible puts in place. His role will be a target in the enemy's sites. For generations, God has faithfully nurtured the men in his family so that their influence would help your husband become a man you can depend on. And Satan has been waging war against what God has been building.

Check your expectations here. Your dad, stepdad, uncle, and grandfather may have offered protection and provision much differently than the man you married. Differences will matter as much as you let them. You can embrace it as an adventure or resist it in fear.

You will set the tone in your home. As you communicate your needs and your expectations to your husband, you can offer him confidence that he can be a great provider with God's help. Or you can fill his mind with your doubts and watch his hope of being someone you respect plummet.

Be on guard for the expectations your parents and his are speaking into your life. They will most likely mean well and want the very best for you. But this is not their marriage. You have chosen to leave their authority and cleave to each other.

Satan is the prince of the air. Watch your thoughts for what your parents "might" say. A threat of a problem may be whispered in hopes that you will take the bait and let worry riddle your mind.

The same enemy will be toying with your parents, luring them to worry about your finances and your neighborhood and how safe your car is. Your work here is to recognize the enemy's tactics and remember, "We do not wrestle against flesh and blood, but against the rulers, against the authorities, against the cosmic powers over this present darkness, against the spiritual forces of evil in the heavenly places" (Ephesians 6:12). Satan will want you to wrestle with your spouse and your parents, leading you to believe they are the enemy. It is actually his plan at work to cause division.

I was Daddy's little girl, and I didn't grow up understanding the concept of healthy boundaries. Even if I had, transitioning from 20-plus years of one provider and protector to another brings the prospect of bumps in the road.

I fell for "imaginations" that Dad would disapprove of my husband's decisions far too many times. There were significant consequences to choosing what my dad thought over my husband's decisions. But at the time, the power of my dad's opinion weighed more. Without realizing it, I was failing to cleave to my husband and exposing my mind and my marriage to the enemy. Satan was playing so many angles trying to destroy my marriage. I was unaware that Dad and David both were wrestling with their own fears, insecurities, and imaginations.

One of God's many roles in your life is provider. Knowing God as a faithful provider to you and your spouse brings peace to your heart and home. As you read the following verse, ask yourself if you believe God is able and willing to provide for you this way.

> Look at the birds of the air: they neither sow nor reap nor gather into barns, and yet your heavenly Father feeds them. Are you not of more value than they? (Matthew 6:26).

God, your Father, also offers protection. As brides, we wear armor God Himself provides as we relate to Him personally, intimately. Our protector is able to defend us against evil and unwise decisions. Our role is to accept His leadership and fall under authority, inviting Him to be the provider and protector of your marriage.

Every good and perfect gift is from God (James 1:17). He is able to deliver your protection and provision through your husband. If your husband struggles, God is there. If your husband strays from God's authority, God is there.

Praying for your husband as your protector and provider is your role as his helpmate. You are engaged in this battle. Take your battle posture of standing on the truths of who God created him to be, who God is, and what God can do. And never stop praying.

Prayer Prompt

Thank You, Father, for being my ultimate provider and protector. You knit me together in my mother's womb to need You in this way (Matthew 6:25; Psalm 90:1–2, 138:13).

You are _____'s protector and provider. You are the source of his wisdom and strength to lead us away from danger and into the plenty you have allotted for us. Thank You for being more than enough to lead him. Regardless of any poor examples in his life and the bad choices he might have made, You are his portion (Proverbs 2:6; Psalm 118:14; 2 Corinthians 9:8; Lamentations 3:24).

Gentle Shepherd, I call out to You on _____'s behalf. Paint a remarkable picture of leadership for _____. Use Your Word, teachings, mentors, and more to make his desires match Your own (Psalm 23:1; 2 Timothy 2:2).

I choose to be _____'s encourager. With Your wisdom, I will affirm _____'s leadership in our home. My eyes will see and my mind will feast on things that are admirable, noble, and praiseworthy. When fear of lack and harm knock on the door of my mind, my lips will proclaim Your goodness, Your provision and protection for us. Your love and kindness are better than life itself (1 Thessalonians 5:11; Philippians 4:8; Psalm 63:3).

Show me, Father, if there is fear in my heart regarding _____'s ability to provide for and protect me. Reveal to me any of my thoughts that disagree with the truth about You and Your design for marriage. I want to enjoy marriage the way You planned it for us. Don't let me get in our way (Psalm 55:10; 2 Corinthians 10:5).

Let the light of Your Word eliminate any sin that stands in _____'s way of fulfilling this role. Your grace is enough for any weaknesses or obstacle _____ will encounter (1 Corinthians 4:5; 2 Corinthians 12:9–10).

Let our marriage mirror Your love for the Church in this way (Ephesians 5).

With Jesus' name on my lips, I pray, believing.

Amen

A Wife's Call to Action

Think of at least one way you can encourage your husband in the roles of provider and protector. Prayerfully make a plan to employ that encouragement, inviting God to prepare your husband to receive it as honor and respect.

Chapter 27

Covering His Priorities, Time, and Energy

Let's talk about expectations a little more.

Did you enter this marriage with expectations regarding your husbands' work ethic and schedule? Do you have a dream-come-true idea of how many hours of the day your husband will be available to you, at home or out having fun together? Your husband has similar expectations. Have the two of you talked about them? Have you identified any differences in opinion? Differences are opportunities to build unity. They do not have to lead to problems.

Just in the last few months, I've begun to recognize how much more balanced David's work and play ratio is than my own. I've always admired him for having hobbies. In my childhood home, these priorities were not as balanced. I have trouble putting work down to enjoy life and David doesn't. He's diligent, efficient, and balanced. But to me the differences often felt like a wedge between us. Today, God's given me a new perspective and I see the difference as a gift, helping me to grasp more of a joy-filled life than I have experienced so far.

Your marriage is so unique. No one has or will ever experience marriage the way you two will live it. You and your husband are creating a new normal together. It will be tempting to create a culture that mimics the influencers in your life. Many people will want great things for your careers and your family time. They will advise you based on their own expectations, perspectives, and rules. Let me encourage you to take ALL of these ideas before the Lord in prayer.

God's perspective is the one you need. He alone has complete understanding of your backgrounds, your emotional needs, your financial needs, the employment opportunities, etc. He loves you both and has planned to be your provider, guide, and counselor. Thankfully, when we need wisdom, we can ask God for it. James 1:5 promises that He gives it generously.

There is a very strong condition to asking for and receiving wisdom from God. Every one of us can ask and it will be "liberally" given if we:

- believe that He will give us wisdom
- believe that His Word is full of this wisdom
- act according to and in agreement with His Word, regardless of the conflict we have raging in our minds and the difficult situation we are facing.

If we ask God for His help and do not trust Him enough to do what He says, we should not expect to receive anything from Him. Asking and not acting lands us in the category of double-minded and unstable in all our ways (James 1:6–8).

Friend, I have been this double-minded wife. I took advice from people who were hearers of the Word but not doers of the Word. I had to shut the door on the free advice coming my way if I could not see the fruits of righteousness in that person's life (Galatians 5:22–23). I also had to limit my exposure to these people. In order to guard my heart and protect my mind, I put boundaries on the types of conversations I would have with certain family members.

I had to learn the hard way to fire my feelings. While the world says, "go with your gut" and "follow your heart," the Bible says: "The heart is deceitful above all things, and desperately sick; who can understand it?"(Jeremiah 17:9). Let that truth sink deep into the fibers of your soul. You cannot trust your heart!

As a new wife, your heart might see your husband's work as competition for his attention. He may see it as the way he shows you love. But what if he works too many hours and you see how it drains him? What if the people he works for don't appreciate him? Will the potential lowliness of his job embarrass you?

Many things about his work can cause you to harbor resentment and bitterness toward the man desiring to serve you as a provider (Hebrews 12:15). Guard your heart (Proverbs 4:23) and protect your marriage by seeking God's wisdom in prayer and living a life of obedience.

Marriage is God's design. God knows the time you and your husband need together. God knows the sacrifices required to spend this quality time together. The rest from work and responsibilities that you both need is known by God. All the answers for your work, your marriage, and your rest are in His hand. All you have to do is ask God for wisdom and be brave enough to do what He says.

Prayer Prompt

Father, You are the Provider of our needs. Thank You for loving me and _____ in this very tangible way (Philippians 4:19).

I am grateful that you have chosen to love me, provide for me financially, and emotionally encourage me through my husband, _____. I receive _____'s commitment to me as provider as a gift of love from You (Ephesians 5:25).

I look forward to depending on You for our income, because You are faithful. Thank You for having a good plan for _____'s future as a provider for us. Thank You for knowing well in advance where he will work, what he will do, whom he will work for and with. It is comforting to know that You have planned for him, and You are walking with him (Deuteronomy 7:9; Jeremiah 29:11; Psalm 139:1–6).

Thank you for creating _____ with passion, personality, and specific talents that can be used to serve employers, industries, and the Church. I invite You to use _____ to accomplish more in his work than either of us have imagined or thought to ask of You. We believe that Your Holy Spirit within _____ supplies him with power, love, and self-discipline. Because of You, he can work fearlessly, knowing You are at work within him (Romans 12:5–8; Ephesians 3:20; 2 Timothy 1:7).

Father, I know that _____ needs affirmation and encouragement in the workplace. You've promised that Your grace and mercy will follow _____ all the days of his life. I ask that You provide the Christian influences, encouragers, and others who will speak blessings over _____ as he works (Psalm 23:6; Matthew 7:7).

Lead _____ away from the temptation to work for the approval of people but to instead work as an act of worship to You. Deliver him, Lord, from the evil that will certainly entice him to work too much or too little at the expense of his health and our marriage. I invite You to be his personal coach in this area and to bring mentors and accountability to help him navigate these choices (Matthew 6:13; Romans 12:1; James 1:14–15; Colossians 2:8; John 16:13; Proverbs 27:17; Galatians 6:1–2).

Only You, God, know the rhythm of time _____ needs to dedicate to work, to our marriage, serving You in other relationships, and rest. Regardless of the pressures _____ might experience, I know that You are able to empower him to choose to prioritize his time. You are his wonderful counselor. Your wisdom and revelation will be his guide. He will trust in You, and be led by Your Word (Ecclesiastes 3; Acts 1:8; Ephesians 1:17, 3:16; Isaiah 9:6; Psalm 118:8, 119:105).

Shepherd me, God, to be a wife who respects her husband's efforts at home and at work. Use me as a voice of joy, hope, and understanding. Guide me to be a wife that speaks truth in love from a heart that desires to remain his number one fan. Let Your love for him flow through me to encourage him and to cover a multitude of sins (Psalm 23:1; Ephesians 4:15, 5:33; 1 Corinthians 13:7; John 15:13; Thessalonians 5:11; 1 Peter 4:8).

Teach _____ and me to observe Your Sabbath. Strengthen us in our love for You and trust in Your Word as our guide so that we can live this out. Guide us to schedule time away from media and anything else in our lives that keeps us from being still in Your presence. We desire to apply Your Word to our lives in this way. Because we trust in Your instructions, we will not grow weary. Your yoke is easy and Your burden is light (Psalm 25:5, 28:7, 46:10; Deuteronomy 5:12; Mark 6:31; James 1:22; Isaiah 40:31; Matthew 11:30).

As for me and _____, we will serve You, our Lord (Joshua 24:15).

In the name of Jesus, I pray.

Amen!

☙ A Wife's Call to Action ❧

Remember the sabbath day, to keep it holy (Exodus 20:8).

Take some time to discuss the fourth commandment with your husband. How important do each of you feel the Sabbath rest is to God and to your marriage?

Chapter 28

Consecrating His Body as God's Temple

Marrying a man who has said "Yes" to a life devoted to Jesus means you said "Yes" to loving, respecting, and helping the temple of God.

Let that thought sit with you awhile.

The Spirit of God dwells within your husband. He is a sacred (set apart for God) man.

> But he who is joined to the Lord becomes one spirit with him. . . . Or do you not know that your body is a temple of the Holy Spirit within you, whom you have from God? You are not your own (1 Corinthians 6:17–19).

If you married someone who has not yet said "Yes" to Jesus, I am agreeing with you that he will. God is able to move mountains, and He is certainly able to move your man to radical dependence on Himself.

When I was a little girl, I was taught to respect the church building because it belonged to God. We wore our Sunday best to God's house. The church building was dedicated to serve an epic purpose and we respected it as such.

Things. We can so easily make them more important than people and the Holy God that lives within them. The church building was and is certainly precious because it is used for God's purposes. But the Body of Christ, the temple of His Holy Spirit, now lives in people. You and your husband are the Church. Your bodies (your lives) are sacred. You are the helpmate of a living sacrifice, holy and acceptable to God (Romans 12:1).

Your husband's consecration (declaration as sacred) occurred supernaturally when he accepted the reality and gift of Jesus. As his most intimate friend and encourager, your role is to reflect this reality to him and pray for him.

How will you talk to him in a way that says, "You are a chosen and sacred priest in God's Kingdom?" How can your conversations about him cause people to see him as God's treasured possession?

Will you look beyond the imperfections that you see in this world and celebrate what is very real about him in God's world? I want you to know that you can. God lives in you. He is ready to empower you to see your man through His eyes, to see him as sacred.

God's enemy is certainly going to attack anything set apart to God's service. There will always be schemes to keep your man from believing and living as if he is set apart to serve God. When you see it happening, you could choose to react in fear and disbelief that your husband would fall for something like that. Or you could respond to the discernment God has given you by praying. You can go boldly to God's throne and ask God to help him. You can ask God to deliver him from the subtle hints of evil you have detected. You can ask God to help you to stand strong against the enemy's plan to cause division between you.

Inviting God to help him give up his self-life so that he can live fully surrendered could be your ultimate calling. God appointed you. As you focus your attention on praying for your husband, God will faithfully guide your prayers to accomplish what He has planned for your husband. The unfolding of His plan in your man will delight your soul. He will implant in your spirit glimpses of what is to come. Hold them close. Write them down. God intends to bring it to pass, and your job is to believe that He can and He will — regardless of what you might see today or next year.

Prayer Prompt

Father, I am amazed by the truth that _____ and I are consecrated to your service. It is a big concept and difficult to grasp. I choose to believe and celebrate it as our reality (1 Corinthians 6:11–20).

_____'s life is yours. On his behalf, I offer his body, mind, skills, and dreams back to You. Thank You for Your forever plan to use him to bring glory to Your name (Jeremiah 29:11).

Help me and _____ want what You want for him. Help us both desire obedience to You more than the wisdom the world offers. Help us to realize the difference (1 Samuel 15:22; James 3:13–16).

I lift up _____'s mind to You. Be the Lord over his thoughts and his desires. Let his mind be set on You and Your Kingdom (Colossians 3:2; Philippians 2:5).

I give you his eyes. Help him to see through the lens of Your truth. With Your love for him, guide his eyes to things that are pure and noble. Keep them from pornography and the lewdness this world offers. Grant him Your supernatural focus on our marriage. Let his eyes find joy and satisfaction when he sees me (Hebrews 12:2; 2 Samuel 11; Proverbs 5:18).

I give you his ears. Guard them from the seductive call of all that is not sacred. Let nothing distract him from the sound of Your voice and the calling You have placed on his life (Psalm 85:8).

I give you his mouth. Fill it, Lord, with praises to You. Allow his voice to transport Your wisdom. Let his words be filled with Your faith, hope, and love (Psalm 19:14, 145:1–2; 1 Corinthians 2:7, 13:13).

I offer to you his organs, tissues, cells, and every system at work in his body. Let them function in the perfection You created them to function. His life and health come from You (Psalm 30:2).

Here are his hands, Lord. Use them for Your service. Let them build up the kingdom and never be used to tear it down. Help him to keep them open toward You so that he is able to receive Your gifts (1 Corinthians 6:20).

Here are his legs and feet, Lord. Guide him to walk in the light of Your truth, always toward You and never away from You. Shepherd him to pursue peace in all his relationships. Ignite within him a fire to deliver the beautiful message of Your gospel to the world around him and wherever you want him to go (1 John 1:7; Hebrews 12:14; Isaiah 52:7).

Let _____'s entire life be filled with the joy that comes from being set apart to serve You (Psalm 100:2).

In the mighty name of Jesus, I pray.

Amen

⤸ A Wife's Call to Action ⤺

Look for an opportunity to tell your husband that you celebrate his life as one set apart to enjoy life with God.

If he has not chosen to devote his life to Jesus yet, find a friend who will pray with you in faith that God is going to accomplish that in his life.

Chapter 29

Satisfying His Needs for Physical Intimacy

God created men with a strong desire for physical intimacy. Okay, I can hear you saying, "Well, *duh*, Jennifer." And you might be thinking, "Hey, I've got a pretty strong desire going on here too!" To that I say, "Hallelujah!"

Here's the thing. Men and women don't always place the same importance on intercourse. There are plenty of resources available to help you sort this out. I want you to do some research on this because the differences could create an "I'm waiting on you to meet my needs first" scenario. Husbands and wives are to be united as one, but our differences make this area of our marriage prime real estate for spiritual battle. When our "serve me" flags fly at full mast, God's enemy is happy to support and defend our point of view.

Remember the concept of oneness with God is demonstrated to the world in marriage. The Bride of Christ is the Church. Saying "Yes" to Jesus means you are brought into a union, a oneness, with Him. This means when God looks at you, He sees Jesus' perfection and accepts you into His presence with great delight. So we can see that the physical act of oneness in marriage is a sacred reflection of our spiritual unity with Christ. Satan, who would like to destroy every beautiful thing from God and about God, has monumental reasons for waging war in the physical union of marriage. To lose our delight in knowing our spouse so intimately can give birth to sin and its devastating consequences. Adultery, pornography, and other sins against your own body (and your husband's) will be readily available opportunities. Each of these brings destruction into your life and the Kingdom of God in your midst. It's a vicious scheme to make God look weak and untrustworthy.

Physical intimacy is very likely the primary way your man desires to connect with you. Of the five love languages taught by Dr. Gary Chapman (gifts, quality time, words of affirmation, acts of service, and physical touch), your man will likely identify physical touch as the primary way he desires to experience love from you. But don't take my word for it. Ask him. His way of defining and expressing intimacy is yours to discover and enjoy.

It is also an opportunity for you to serve him sacrificially. Yes, I just referred to sexual intimacy with your husband as a sacrifice. I'm smiling right now thinking about how ridiculous that sounds to you as a new bride. You are married and finally free to enjoy his body without being disobedient to God and I'm calling this a sacrifice. Go ahead, laugh. Get it out of your system. Tweet it if you want. But hear me out.

One day, your untrustworthy heart (Jeremiah 17:9) will start a conversation with you that will sound something like this:

> He wants me to have sex? Now? Are you kidding me? He hasn't _____ OR _____. I have been _____ and _____ and he really wants sex right now! Good Grief!

How are you going to handle your heart's cry for fairness and a little sensitivity? Trust me when I tell you that your entitled feeling will be met with some encouragement from the enemy of your marriage. He will rush to defend your feelings and give you excuses for not participating until _____ happens.

God, however, has given us clear direction on this subject. He knows everything about you and He is for you. He is the supplier of all your needs. And He wants you to live like this:

> But because of the temptation to sexual immorality, each man should have his own wife and each woman her own husband. The husband should give to his wife her conjugal rights, and likewise the wife to her husband. **For the wife does not have authority over her own body**, but the husband does. Likewise the husband does not have authority over his own body, but the wife does. Do not deprive one another, except perhaps by agreement for a limited time, that you may devote yourselves to prayer; but then come together again, **so that Satan may not tempt you because of your lack of self-control** (1 Corinthians 7:2–5, emphasis mine).

God says your man has authority over your body. He also says that you are not to deprive your husband in order to protect your marriage from the very real temptations Satan has planned for him. This is your own personal responsibility. Yes, God gave your Mr. Forever responsibilities as well.

Invite God into every conversation you and your husband have about sexual intimacy. Ask Him to give both of you wisdom and a heart of obedience to His Word on the subject. Without God's intervention, this area of giving and submission in your marriage can become a battlefield.

God wants this for your husband:

> Enjoy life with the wife whom you love, all the days of your vain life that he has given you under the sun, because that is your portion in life (Ecclesiastes 9:9).

> Let your fountain be blessed, and rejoice in the wife of your youth, a lovely deer, a graceful doe. Let her breasts fill you at all times with delight; be intoxicated always in her love (Proverbs 5:18–19).

You are the wife God has given him to enjoy. God designed him to be intoxicated by your love. It is a beautiful design for marriage and an extraordinary purpose for you as a wife.

You have the opportunity to partner with God to protect this gift. God is able to protect it. Just remember, a very real spiritual enemy is always opposing our God and all that He wants for you. **God never fails.** But your free will is a critical factor in the outcome.

Trust me in this — Satan does not wish for you to satisfy your husband's desires. He will not suggest ideas that will lead you to delight in sexual intercourse God's way. He will be ready to encourage you about your rights and what you deserve. He will never recommend you sacrifice your needs and wants for what your husband needs. He will surely be taunting your husband with other seemingly satisfying opportunities. He will distort God's truth and whisper it to both of you at your most vulnerable moments.

Let's talk about vulnerability. If you find that intercourse with your husband causes you to feel "too physically or emotionally vulnerable," take this to God in prayer. You may have already been injured on the spiritual battlefield in this area. God knows what happened. He understands your reaction. He is your source of health and healing. He wants you to enjoy all that He offers you in marriage. He knows how to help you. Follow His lead and seek the biblical counsel of those He highlights as His choice for you.

Presenting your body to your husband is an act of obedience and therefore, an act of worshiping God (Romans 12:1). This truth has become my reality as I have sought God for the healing in this area of my marriage. Satan's plans to destroy my marriage were at work long before I ever said "I do." The sexual sins I willingly and unwillingly participated in caused brokenness that greatly affected this area of my marriage to David, and my first marriage to Michael. Now, I have a greater understanding of God's truth behind these verses:

> Flee from sexual immorality. Every other sin a person commits is outside the body, but the sexually immoral person sins against his own body. Or do you not know that

your body is a temple of the Holy Spirit within you, whom you have from God? You are not your own, for you were bought with a price. So glorify God in your body (1 Corinthians 6:18–20).

The Bible tells us that the wages of sin is death and that includes sexual sin (Romans 6:23). The enemy employed sexual sins in his strategy to destroy both my marriages. Be assured that his plan to destroy your marriage will likely include sexual sin. But because of Jesus, you and your husband have the power to avoid temptation, to overcome the devastations, to enjoy healing, and the beautiful intimacy God designed for your delight. God's power resurrected Jesus from the dead. His power is surely able to resurrect the dead places in you, your husband, and your relationship. God is able.

I'm speaking from experience here. God is able. He has done this for me and He is happy to do it for everyone. This area of marriage has been one of the best gospel teachers for me. I've learned the sacrifice of giving love, feeling inept to fulfill my husband's desire, and trusting God to love him through me. As I anticipate our time together, I prayerfully offer my body and the gift of my willingness to God as an act of worship.

You can trust that God's call for you to lavish love onto your husband through sexual intimacy is ultimately going to bring you great joy throughout your long life together. Your passion may ebb and flow, your body may change with the years, but these three things remain: faith, hope, and love. And the greatest of these is love (1 Corinthians 13:13).

Prayer Prompt

Holy Father, Your design for marriage is so beautiful and intricately woven into my relationship with You. Thank You for revealing this to me in Your Word. Thank You for being present with me and helping me understand Your best for me and _____ in our physical act of love (2 Corinthians 11:2; Psalm 119:105; Matthew 28:20; John 14:26).

I am honored you chose me to bring great delight to my husband, _____. This beautiful role you have given me is exciting. While I do not understand all of the "hows" and "whys" of it, I trust that You do. I am willing to learn what You want me to know about _____ and his needs for physical affection and intercourse. And I am willing to be shepherded by You while I am learning. Thank You, God, for being constant and faithful to me (Ecclesiastes 9:9; John 10:27; 2 Thessalonians 3:3).

I want what You want for _____. Thank You for giving him good and satisfying gifts and leading me to do the same. Help me to be generous toward _____ with my body and my affections. Use me as a vessel through which You pour out on _____ the blessings You want for him (Psalm 37:4; James 1:17; Luke 6:38; 2 Corinthians 4:7).

Your enemy, and the enemy of our marriage, would like to destroy the good gift of my physical love for _____. I am aware that this is a serious battle and one that I cannot fight alone. Help me, God. Help me to listen and obey You. Protect me in the spiritual and physical realm from the temptation to withhold my love. Help me to hear Your voice leading me. Grant me the courage to follow You instead of my own fleshly desires (John 10:10, 27; Psalm 121:2, 7; Matthew 6:13; 1 Corinthians 7:4–5; Galatians 5:17–18).

Jesus, bring hope and healing where the enemy has already stolen from us in this area. Send Your Word, Your trustworthy people, and resources into our lives to lead us along Your paths of righteousness (Isaiah 61:1–4; Psalm 107:20; Proverbs 4:11).

Let nothing stand between our physical union so that the world will know of Your perfect, sacrificial, and fulfilling love (1 John 3:16, 4:18).

For Your glory, Lord, I ask You for these things in Jesus' name.

Amen

A Wife's Call to Action

Have an open and honest conversation with your husband about pornography. Discuss both of your experiences with it and your views of it.

Take some time to confess the sin of pornography to God.

Create a contract with each other to remove any possibility of pornography being a part of your marriage experience.

Guarding the Prize

He who has learned to pray has learned the greatest secret of a holy and happy life.[17]

— William Law

. . . love as distinct from "being in love" — is not merely a feeling. It is deep unity, maintained by will and deliberately strengthened by habit; reinforced by (in Christian marriage) the grace which both partners ask and receive from God. . . . "Being in love" first moved them to promise of fidelity: this quieter love enables them to keep the promise. It is on this love that the engine of marriage is run: being in love was the explosion that started it.[18]

— C.S. Lewis

Chapter 30

Nourish: Becoming a Captive Audience

The Bible is your hope. Without a steady diet of It, you could lose the spiritual and physical battle for your marriage. Being a hearer of the Word is not going to be enough for you to remain standing under the attacks that are certainly going to come your way. Going to church, hearing a great sermon, singing your favorite hymns and praise songs will help. But unless you are feeding yourself more of Jesus than the other things of this world, you will fall victim to the schemes the enemy launches at you.

Do you believe that?

Psalm 119 sets the example of living in God's Word, trusting it is the truth, acting on it, and finding joy because of it. Nothing in this world will supply you and your husband with more perfect advice. No one will offer you more comfort. No other book, seminar, or subscription will rescue you from your sinful nature. The Word of God is alive. As each of you read, think, and talk about the Bible, the mysterious miracle of change is ignited. It will transform your mind and then your life into the "new creation" Jesus died to give you. It will guide you out of the drama your selfish nature would otherwise choose to create.

The embarrassing mistakes and heavy burdens in my marriages were born out of a puny diet on God's truth. So many times we thought we were doing right until we learned God's Word said something different. It became apparent to me that failure was being born out of what I thought I knew.

Look at the promise in Psalm 119:5–6:

> Oh that my ways may be steadfast in keeping your statutes! Then I shall not be put to shame, having my eyes fixed on all your commandments.

As brides, we surely do not want to live in shame and we do not want that for our husbands. We certainly do not want to endure the shame of divorce, adultery, imprisonment, etc. How can we protect ourselves? Verses 5 and 6 tell us to be steadfast in keeping God's statutes (permanent rules) and THEN we will not be put to shame.

What would shame in marriage look like to you?

Now not all rough patches in your marriage are going to be the result of your personal sins. You cannot live in such a righteous bubble that you will be immune to the work of the enemy around you. Very hard days, months, or years could happen at the hand of another. Injustice is prevalent and we are not exempt.

The Psalmist teaches us to look for comfort and even life in God's promises.

> This is my comfort in my affliction, that your promise gives me life (Psalm 119:50).

The Word of God will satisfy you more than a Pinterest-worthy home. It will satisfy you more than a closet full of name brands for every season. It will satisfy you more than the attention you want from people. It will satisfy you when your heart is broken and when tomorrow is very uncertain.

The law of your mouth is better to me than thousands of gold and silver pieces (Psalm 119:72).

How sweet are your words to my taste, sweeter than honey to my mouth! (Psalm 119:103).

Your testimonies are my heritage forever, for they are the joy of my heart (Psalm 119:111).

Within Psalm 119 you will also find the Psalmist reminding God that he has kept the law and lived in obedience to God's statutes. When he is in trouble and crying out to God for help, he reminds God of his personal faithfulness. What good could that do? Is he bragging? Negotiating with God?

There are promises associated with obeying God, and the Psalmist was reminding God of His own promises. The Sovereign God who planned an abundant life for you is still there to help you enjoy it regardless of the evil around you. He promises that choosing His way will make you prosperous and successful (Deuteronomy 29:9; Joshua 1:8). Prosperity and success is defined by God and certainly not by our culture.

I'm inviting you to humble yourself and all that you think you know about life under the authority of God, the giver of life. Choose His way over your own. Take one step in pursuit of His way and then another. If you take this chance on Him, in time you will reap the joyful marriage your mind has imagined. Actually, you will have more joy and peace than you could ever have dreamed possible (Ephesians 3:20). He is for you. He is faithful. And His Word will never return empty, but will always accomplish His intentions (Isaiah 55:11). You can trust that His intentions for your marriage are GOOD!

Dedicate yourself to an intimate relationship with God. With His Word, He will tell you everything you need to know about Him. Your intimacy with God will infuse life into your marriage. Your husband's intimacy with God will do the same. Imagine the results of time in His Word together.

Prayer Prompt

Generous God,

You have given us Your Word as our instruction manual for life together. We choose to study it and apply it to every area of our marriage. Thank You for offering us a no-fail, how-to guide for a "shame-free" life and marriage. We will feast on Your message to us for the rest of our days (Psalm 119:4, 5, 103).

The song of our marriage will be praise and thanksgiving to You. As we focus on You and Your ways, our hearts will be encouraged. Regardless of our circumstances, our joy in being Yours will remain strong (Psalm 119:7, 54, 62, 108).

Let the truths in Your Word tear down every stronghold that pollutes our hearts and minds. Replace in us every wrong way of thinking with Your thoughts. Without Your gift of truth, we would drown in our own sin and problems. Your message to us brings life to every dark and desperate place (Psalm 119:9, 11, 92, 93, 107).

We are in awe that You, God, are our teacher. We will say what You say and do what Jesus did. We invite Your Holy Spirit living in us to open our spiritual eyes to see You and know Your awesomeness in these Scriptures. Our hearts will delight to do what You have instructed over the pursuit of money or any other desire (Psalm 119:12–14, 18, 37; Philippians 2:5).

We will rely on You to counsel us through Your Word. We trust that following your instructions will ultimately bring renewal and joy (Psalm 119:24, 50, 107).

With all of our hearts, we want to please You. Thank You for the generous portion of mercy You dole out to us when we trip on our own desires. We are hidden from real harm by You. Our security lies in the power of Your Word (Psalm 119:58, 114).

We crave the company of those who love Your Word and live by it. By Your divine design, those who love You will be drawn to us and enjoy our company. Because of our trust in You, we will not be associated with or influenced by those who walk outside of Your light (Psalm 119:63, 74, 79, 105, 113, 115, 130).

Of all the complete and beautiful things You have shown us, nothing compares to Your perfection. Wow! How incredible to know You and enjoy a life together exploring Your unlimited goodness (Psalm 119:96).

To You be the glory for our marriage forever.

Amen

A Wife's Call to Action

Consider the shame involved in the marriage of someone you know or have read about recently. Which of God's laws have been broken? Who broke them?

How could living according to God's Word restore the unity and intimacy in that marriage? What Bible verses point to the hope that marriage needs?

Find within Psalm 119 one verse that you want to live out in your marriage and make it prominent in your home.

Chapter 31

Cement the Experience of Unity

"What God has joined together, let no man separate" is said at most weddings. It is not just a popular saying found in wedding books for preachers. It is from the mouth of Jesus.

"... and the two shall become one flesh." So they are no longer two but one flesh. What therefore God has joined together, let not man separate (Mark 10:8–9).

Oneness in Marriage

Do you know what that means? To be honest, I did not. My mother-in-law was the first person who made the concept real for me. She was sharing marriage wisdom she had employed over the last 60 years of marriage. She explained that talking negatively about your husband was a slap in the face to yourself because the two of you are one. I was taken aback by her comment. *Are you?*

As a Christian, you represent Christ. People evaluate what they see you and other Christians do and make a character judgment about God. It seems a little unfair for Jesus since we are not sinless and He is.

Christ's love for His Bride, His Church, is so deep and pure that it goes much deeper than His reputation. He gave up His reputation so that we would have the same access to God that He has. He endured torture and mockery to accomplish it. And He knew we would not be able to do as much for Him as He did for us. But He still wanted us.

Christ Jesus nourishes and cherishes His Bride because we are members of His Body.

> In the same way husbands should love their wives as their own bodies. He who loves his wife loves himself. For no one ever hated his own flesh, but nourishes and cherishes it, just as Christ does the church, because we are members of his body. "Therefore a man shall leave his father and mother and hold fast to his wife, and the two shall become one flesh" (Ephesians 5:28–31).

One Body

In the eyes of God, you and Mr. Forever are also members of the same body now. Becoming one flesh is consummated in the marriage bed. But it does not end there, just as life with Christ does not end after baptism. Jesus pursues a present-tense love relationship with His Church. You said "I do" to the very same lifestyle of enduring, pursuing love and oneness. Your oneness with your husband will always be a present-tense pursuit.

One Mind

> So if there is any encouragement in Christ, any comfort from love, any participation in the Spirit, any affection and sympathy, complete my joy by being of the same mind, having the same love, being in full accord and of one mind (Philippians 2:1–2).

It is possible to love and work together with one mind and one purpose. The Spirit of Christ lives in you to make sure you can do it. It may take longer than you hoped, but it can be greater than you imagined.

Division is a tool in the hand of the enemy. Even the Church struggles to stay united. Paul started his letter to the Corinthians addressing it.

> I appeal to you, brothers, by the name of our Lord Jesus Christ, that all of you agree, and that there be no divisions among you, but that you be united in the same mind and the same judgment (1 Corinthians 1:10).

You and your husband can share life together united by the mind of Christ (1 Corinthians 2:16). You will face opportunities to be divided on many topics. But you are united as one by Jesus, the One who tells us to not let any man divide what God has joined.

One Spirit

Maybe today you are filled with deep concern that you and your husband are "unequally yoked." That means one of you is not living with God as your Lord and Master (2 Corinthians 6:14). You are not alone, friend. Many women are devoted to God while their husbands are not yet there.

Connie B., one of my marriage mentors, has faced this too. Here's her story:

> As a young wife, following Christ was not my top priority. As time passed, the Holy Spirit drew me back to Himself. However, I was concerned about taking that step toward spiritual growth and "leaving my husband behind." The Lord spoke to my heart with these words, "You follow Me and leave your husband to Me." That was not easy, friend.
>
> I would "help the Holy Spirit out" sometimes and, surprisingly, my husband would get angry. I was "preaching" to him.
>
> As I tearfully and frequently sought the Lord in prayer, He showed me a better way. His Way! He showed me the verse in 1 Peter 3:1 that says, "Likewise, wives, be subject to your own husbands, so that even if some do not obey the

word, they may be won without a word by the conduct of their wives."

You know what that required, right? I had to shut my mouth, and consistently live out my faith in front of him! That required a lot of prayer for him, and me. It took a little while, but it worked. My husband became a believer in the Lord Jesus Christ! No more preaching from me, and no more fighting between us, when I did it God's way.

Do you see the spiritual attack in Connie B's experience? She wanted to please God by living in unity with her husband. Where do you think the fear of leaving her husband behind spiritually came from? It sounds logical, doesn't it? But God's ways and thoughts extend beyond our human reasoning (Isaiah 55:8–9). We must listen to God, our commander, and be always ready to say "Yes, Lord," even when our minds argue with the next step (2 Corinthians 10:5).

Their spiritual unity began when he became one with Christ. They are equally yoked. Connie's choice to do marriage God's way was pivotal in this victory and their 45 years of life as one.

Christ made a way for His Church to be united, and He is ready to make a way for you and your husband.

Prayer Prompt

Oh God of the Holy Trinity,

You gave us Jesus, whose entire life encourages oneness with You. You've given _____ and me Your Spirit so that we can have all the help we need to know You, to think like You, and to imitate You (1 John 5:20; 2 Corinthians 1:22; 1 Corinthians 2:16, 11:1).

Churches divide and families separate — all evidence that You are opposed (Romans 6:17–18).

But we live in Your Kingdom under Your authority with Jesus interceding for us. Your Word lights our path and joins our minds (Matthew 6:9–10; Romans 8:34; Psalm 119:105).

I declare that the same power that raised Jesus from the dead is fighting for me and _____ so that we live together operating as one (Ephesians 1:19–23; 1 Corinthians 1:10).

Let the challenges of life push us forward into total dependence on You to remain together. You hold the world in Your hands. You are our mighty fortress, a safe place to rest and transform into Your likeness (Psalm 18:2, 119:71; Colossians 1:17; 2 Corinthians 3:18).

Thank You for every evidence of Your generous love and character. Your way is reliable and worthy of our trust. We trust that taking up our cross and laying down our lives for each other will lead to an amazing life of love together (1 John 4:9–12, 19; Luke 9:23).

This world needs more examples of unity. Help us be a bright one.

I pray this in Jesus' name, for Your glory.

Amen

A Wife's Call to Action

Are you an equally yoked bride? Does your husband love and serve the Lord selflessly and sacrificially? Is he leading you to do the same?

If you answered yes, take a few moments to praise God for this incomparable gift. Extend your praise to God for this gift by telling your husband how thankful you are.

If you answered no, decide today not to live despairing but with hope. The enemy will fiercely oppose your hope. But God will give you courage and strength while He works to bring about the unity you long for.

Your prayers for your husband will open the doors of heaven, releasing all God wants for him into his life.

Nellie, a wife and mother of two adult children, is ready to encourage you with her own experience. Go to prayersfornewbrides. com/chapter31 and learn how she prayed for her husband.

Chapter 32

Declare a Peace-filled Home

There are so many divorce stories that include the statements, "I hated pulling into the driveway of our home" and "I never knew which wife I was coming home to, the one I dated or the one that lives there now."

Men are wired by God to receive respect from their wives. Just as God desires to be honored and recognized for who He is and what He has done, so does your husband. How will you honor him when your feelings are on fire?

How peaceful was the home you grew up in? Were arguments the norm? Was there an air of contention in the home? Were problems ignored while people seethed in anger?

Friend, many events in your life and your marriage could be used to justify being a quarrelsome and fretful woman. You have the freedom to do it. But there is a cost associated with your choice.

The Bible tells us that living with an argumentative or quarreling wife is a real nightmare.

> . . . a wife's quarreling is a continual dripping of rain (Proverbs 19:13).

> It is better to live in a corner of the housetop than in a house shared with a quarrelsome wife (Proverbs 21:9).

It is better to live in a desert land than with a quarrelsome and fretful woman (Proverbs 21:19).

Are your feelings usually in charge of guiding your behavior and decisions? Your feelings are important indicators given to you by God. But God did not recommend you let them lead.

The heart is deceitful above all things, and desperately sick; who can understand it? (Jeremiah 17:9).

Katie, a young wife and dear friend, offers this wisdom on feelings and marriage:

We are living in the "me" generation. A generation built on feelings. Can I be honest? NEVER TRUST YOUR FEELINGS. The way you feel today, right now in this very moment, will change drastically in a day, month, and year. You cannot trust your feelings because they are emotional. They are not based on what is true. If you ask me, the ONLY thing in this life worth trusting is God's Word. It never fails, it's built on truth, and it is everything pure and good.

She's so right. My feelings of fear, anxiousness, bitterness, and anger have led me to make too many mistakes in my marriage. I've shared with you the times I loosed my anger about David into the lives of others instead of talking it out with him. Because I grew up in a home where confrontation was avoided, I knew no other outlet. I seethed on the inside, destroying the peace in my mind and body and ultimately our marriage. Many women freely release their anger and cause major damage in the hearts of their husbands.

You have a choice.

In hard times, your feelings will want to rule your life. People who truly love you will also advise you according to their feelings. Be very careful not to let God's enemy lead you down a disastrous path because you followed your feelings or theirs.

A life of simple obedience will bring peace to your heart.

> And the effect of righteousness will be peace, and the result of righteousness, quietness and trust forever (Isaiah 32:17).

God poured the truth in Isaiah 32:17 into me very deeply. He used it to turn my ambition and passion into obeying Him because I wanted His promised peace. The simple truth that peace comes from obedience filled my heart and my marriage with hope.

Since then the new creation I had read about in the Bible and heard about in sermons has become more evident in my everyday life. Today I am so different than the girl who married first Michael, then David. My newer friends are shocked when I describe myself as once being bitter and angry. Submitting myself to the authority of God's Word instead of my own thoughts and feelings made the difference.

Maybe your heart and mind are still seeking rest. Maybe peace is just a word to you and not a reality. The answer to the cries of your heart is found in God.

> You keep him in perfect peace whose mind is stayed on you, because he trusts in you (Isaiah 26:3).

> Those who look to him are radiant, and their faces shall never be ashamed (Psalm 34:5).

Let Jesus be your peace coach. He is the Prince of Peace and He is able to "give you peace at all times and in every way" (2 Thessalonians 3:16).

Your peace will be a gift to your husband. Your obedience will defend your sacred union and greatly impact your prayer life.

> The eyes of the Lord are toward the righteous and his ears toward their cry (Psalm 34:15).

> If one turns away his ear from hearing the law, even his prayer is an abomination (Proverbs 28:9).

You are a praying wife. You are confidently standing firm on the promises of God and praying. God answers the prayers of those who are obedient.

Invite God to ready you for this battle with the shoes of peace or feet that are moving forward, not bogged down with a heavy heart of bitterness and resentment.

For he himself is our peace, who has made us both one and has broken down in his flesh the dividing wall of hostility (Ephesians 2:14).

Prayer Prompt

Jesus, I thank You for bringing me and _____ into Your kingdom where peace reigns. I do not want to waste another day giving my emotions a chance to run or ruin my life (Ephesians 2:14; Philippians 4:7; Matthew 6:27; Jeremiah 17:9).

Give me eyes to see anger, bitterness, and jealousy as self-protecting imposters. I trust that You are patient and compassionate. I will not fear the changes You want to make in me. You are merciful. You love me in spite of myself. Help me to embrace this reality (Matthew 13:16; Ephesians 4:31–32; 1 Corinthians 13:4–7; Psalm 103:8, 145:8; 1 John 4:18; Romans 5:8–10).

While the accuser seeks to condemn me, You desire to renew me and transform me. I will follow the footsteps of the Prince of Peace. I will feast at the table of Your Word knowing You are where my help comes from (Revelation 12:10; Romans 12:1–2; Psalm 23:5, 34:8, 46:1).

In obedience to You, I will strive for peace with everyone. My priority is a life of peace with my husband, _____. Help me, Jesus, to plan for peace with him and to live a life of joy (Hebrews 12:14; Proverbs 12:20).

Use me as Your channel of peace in _____'s life. Teach me to nurture a peace-filled marriage and home (John 14:27; Galatians 5:22; 2 Thessalonians 3:16).

I invite you to deliver _____ from everything that seeks to steal the gift of peace You have for him. Let his mind and heart be completely united with You (John 10:10; 1 Corinthians 6:17).

I celebrate Your power to overcome the world and its peace-robbers. Use our marriage to radiate the peace You have to offer the world (John 16:33; Psalm 34:5).

In the name of Jesus, my Prince of Peace, I pray.

Amen

A Wife's Call to Action

We are imitators of Christ. We are called to speak truth in love and work toward peace instead of division.

> Rather, speaking the truth in love, we are to grow up in every way into him who is the head, into Christ (Ephesians 4:15).

Speaking the truth in love might be a very foreign concept to you. It was to me. I'm still learning to think and respond this way.

In John chapter 4, Jesus speaks the truth in love to the Samaritan woman at the well. Reread this encounter and answer the following questions.

1. What was the truth?

2. How did Jesus deliver the truth with love in His heart for this woman, a Samaritan woman that Jews would normally not acknowledge?

3. Has anyone spoken a difficult truth to you in this loving way? If so, ask God to help you use your experience as a model. If not, ask God to bring this experience into your life so that you can learn.

Chapter 33

Communicate as a Team

What is your idea of great communication with your husband? Take a moment and think through what it looks like in your mind to agree, disagree, compromise, and resolve a problem together.

Both of you walked into this marriage with informal training in this area. Maybe it came from movies and television, maybe from your awesome parents that are more in love today than ever. Regardless of where you learned to communicate with a spouse, it's a good bet that the two of you learned differently. You have different parents and influencers, therefore you have differences.

Be assured that God's enemy will target your communication styles. The marriage destroyer would love for you to stop communicating. If you chose to lie to your fella instead of addressing a hard subject, that enemy would host a victory dance.

David and I were conflict avoiders when we married. Together, we made such a mess. We handled anger very differently, and that caused even more conflict. It was so much work to avoid the hard conversation we needed to have. Resentment settled in like a flu virus (maybe mononucleosis in our case) that tainted every aspect of our intimacy. We made "if . . . then" assumptions that produced storm clouds in our thoughts about each other.

Our fears and pride kept the cycle going. This destructive duo kept our attentions and emotions inflamed. Without the distraction, we could have offered each other mercy. We could have approached each other with the attitude, "No matter what, I'm on your team." We could have been open to another point of view with a willingness to admit we might be wrong. Our goal could have been to achieve a great outcome for the united David and Jennifer.

In my mind, being right was more important than being unified. Division was the result.

Are you going to let the need to be right cause division in your marriage? Are you going to let fear, pride, and other self-focused issues destroy the beautiful thing God has joined together?

Are your communication skills healthy? What about your husband's? It is possible you might need to learn a few new approaches. How will you know?

Start by asking God for His perfect perspective, wisdom, and intervention in this area of your life together. Allow Him to coach each of you. Determine to face it as team. There will be challenges. Praise Him for them. Without them, you will not grow to know more about yourself, your spouse, or your God. And you might miss becoming the "perfect and complete" you that God intended for you to mature into.

> Count it all joy, my brothers, when you meet trials of various kinds, for you know that the testing of your faith produces steadfastness. And let steadfastness have its full effect, that you may be perfect and complete, lacking in nothing (James 1:2–4).

With the trials, your view of the world can increase the same way a tune gets better with harmony and variations in rhythm. Imagine listening to one musician for the rest of your life. That's what a marriage ruled by one of your opinions will be. Open your mind to the adventure of idea exploration within the boundaries of God's guidelines.

Allow this incredible marriage relationship to expand your listening skills, your loving skills, and your character as a teammate.

See the two of you standing at the finish line together, clasped hands in the air celebrating victory. Don't allow fear or pride to keep your team from training. Keep your mind on the team instead of yourself. Remember, Jesus set the pace for this race. He modeled for us the sacrifice of His own fame and His rights. He gave. He poured out even more love when He was denied and dismissed. He did what God told Him to do.

That is your responsibility on this team. Do what God tells you to do. He wrote the Book on how to win. You can trust His instructions. Go for it!

Prayer Prompt

God, You are our ultimate example of communicating with a spouse. Your love for the Bride of Christ is evident in Your Words and Your gifts. We want to rely on Your help as we resolve conflicts and make decisions (2 Corinthians 11:2; Psalm 121:2).

Grant us Your wisdom when addressing difficult subjects. Let us see and hear the other's heart with the spiritual wisdom that You freely give. Teach us to speak truth to each other in love. As we navigate these days together, let our words and actions toward the other be compassionate, humble, patient, gentle, and kind (James 1:5; Ephesians 1:18, 4:15; Isaiah 11:2; Colossians 3:12).

We are one. Teach us to think as one, not selfishly or independently. With Your moment-by-moment leadership, we will finish the race together. Every witness to our marriage will see the joy of our surrender to You, Our Lord (Romans 15:5–6; 2 Timothy 4:7; 2 Corinthians 2:14; James 4:7).

Let it be so, for Your glory, Lord.

A Wife's Call to Action

Review God's communication instructions in James 1:19.

> Know this, my beloved brothers: let every person be quick to hear, slow to speak, slow to anger.

Evaluate yourself on each point.

1. Quick to listen
2. Slow to speak
3. Slow to anger

Ask God to reveal the truth to you, the truth from His perspective. He adores you and He knows where you get tripped up and why. He is gentle and kind. He is patient with you and your husband. He's ready to help you both grow in each of these areas. His Spirit in you is ready to strengthen you, quiet you, and give you the words your spouse needs to hear.

Talk to God about it. He is listening.

Chapter 34

Grow the Opportunity to Give Together

The way you and your husband tackle financial decisions can lead to an even greater sense of "oneness" in your marriage. Like communication differences, money decisions can also cause great struggle and lead to division. In fact, your communication skills will certainly affect this area. Decide today to tackle money matters as a team with God as your coach.

The Bible warns that the love of money is a root of all kinds of evils (1 Timothy 6:10). That is a very strong truth. So gear up, soldier girl. Evil can be lurking in the shadows of your hearts.

I highly recommend proactive praying. Don't wait until there is a problem to bring God into this area of your marriage. He sees your situation with perfect vision. He is the strength needed for the weaknesses you both bring to the table.

Do the two of you agree on these things?

1. Work is a form of worship (Colossians 3:17).

2. Wealth and riches come from God (1 Chronicles 29:12).

3. Give the first fruits of your income back to God regardless of your bills and any financial hardship (Proverbs 3:9–10; Malachi 3:10; Luke 21:1–4).

4. The deceitfulness of riches can choke out the power of God's Word in your life (Mark 4:19).

5. Generosity to the poor delights the Lord (Proverbs 19:17).

6. Borrowing money makes you a slave to the lender (Proverbs 22:7).

7. The rich will fade away along with all they have achieved. (James 1:9–11, 5:1–3).

8. God loves a cheerful giver (2 Corinthians 9:7).

9. It is better to give than receive (Acts 20:35).

10. God will supply all that you need (Philippians 4:19).

Hopefully you do. But in case that you've discovered some differences in opinion, do not fear. Lean into God. He is your source of wisdom and has the power to bring unity. This marriage of yours is God's design. He is quite capable of working through each of you to resolve the issues. He wants to because what you do with money reflects back on Him. You wear God's armor and Jesus' name.

Financial challenges can be celebrated. Why? Because the tension delivers a new opportunity to know God better and recognize your need for Him. Each one of us needs to own the humility of needing God if we want to see our marriage flourish and survive the test of the times (Proverbs 16:18).

You and your husband only have to agree with God, seek His help, and do what He tells you to do. That sounds so easy, right? But dying to your own ideas and agreeing with each other and God could take years. Do not despair. God is patient and His Spirit enables you to be, too. God is forgiving and He is alive in you to help you forgive your man and yourself when needed.

God owns the cattle on a thousand hills. He is the ultimate steward of unlimited resources in His heavenly kingdom. He gives and He takes away. He gives, and He gives even more. His purposes are sometimes seen and sometimes intended to be unseen. Invite Him to cause your sacred union to be a fountain of generosity, ready to meet the needs He shows you.

Prayer Prompt

God, I am here to celebrate Your power to provide for all of creation. You tell the sun and the soil how to nourish the fields. You cause the wind to carry the seed. Your world is brimming with plenty (Colossians 1:17).

You are the giver and we are the receivers. Day after day you supply our daily bread and delight our senses with Your living artistry. For every whisper of discontentment that has left these lips, I beg your forgiveness. I choose to live with my eyes wide open to Your faithfulness to provide (Ecclesiastes 2:26; James 1:17; Matthew 6:11; Romans 1:20; 1 Timothy 6:6–7; Philippians 4:19).

The love of money and the evil that comes with it is frightening. I do not want our marriage to fall victim to the trap of wanting more. Sear in our minds Your design for earning, tithing, spending, saving, and giving. Weave into the fabric of our marriage an unbreakable unity. Strengthen our faith in You as our provider and defender. Let every discussion _____ and I have about money be spoken in love. Grant to us both a double portion of 1 Corinthians 13 love so that peace rules our marriage (1 Timothy 6:9–10; Ephesians 4:3; Romans 10:17; 1 Corinthians 13).

The desire of my heart is that _____ and I would become a generous team working for Your purposes, not for our own glory. Purify our hearts in this matter, Lord. Show us our sin. Help us to disregard this world's culture of greed. Set our feet on high ground so that we are always seeing money from Your point of view. Make us willing to be radically different than those close to us who do not follow Your leading (Acts 20:35; Colossians 1:10; Psalm 51:10; Proverbs 28:25).

You own the cattle on a thousand hills. You are our shepherd, and we will not want for any good thing (Psalm 50:10, 23:1).

With Jesus in my heart, I pray.

Amen

❧ A Wife's Call to Action ❧

Do you believe that Jesus' instructions and promise in Luke 6:38 are true for you?

> Give, and it will be given to you. Good measure, pressed down, shaken together, running over, will be put into your lap. For with the measure you use it will be measured back to you (Luke 6:38).

Have you seen this principle in action in your own life or the lives of others?

Do you and your husband trust God as your provider?

Spend at least 20 minutes journaling about your faith in God as your provider and how that affects your spending and giving.

Chapter 35

Employ Healthy Boundaries

Every married couple is the product of two sets of unique backgrounds, personalities, and quirks. Since you are both flawed humans, your union is a beautiful mess in need of the One who handles messes flawlessly.

But why do we need healthy boundaries, who do we need them with, and why? Dr. Henry Cloud and Dr. John Townsend are relationship boundary authors and experts. They define a boundary as "a personal property line that marks those things for which we are responsible."[19] These boundaries are critical in marriage because we remain two individuals who have become one in marriage. We are still responsible for our own thoughts and opinions, our emotions, and our relationship with God. Being married does not ensure we always agree or feel the same about important issues.

Unhealthy boundaries take the form of control and passivity. They either demand too much responsibility or they give too much responsibility. Ultimately, they erode the true concepts of love and honor, our responsibilities in marriage. God is the standard we should look to as we check our own boundaries. He has given us the freedom to love and honor Him but He does not demand it. He knows what is right for us but He doesn't force it on us. The

Creator of relationships sets the bar for personal responsibility in our relationships.

I have really struggled with personal boundaries in my relationships. As I write this, God is revealing to me the need for growth I have in this area. My automatic response has been passive in relationships with men. Fear and laziness are tangled in the why. Generations of women in my family have been passive, allowing their husbands too much freedom in dictating thoughts and actions. But regardless of my experiences, I am responsible for pursuing the balance God intends.

Do you lean more toward control or passivity in your relationships?

It will be much easier to see the flaws in your husband's boundaries than your own. We are usually blind to our own issues, thanks to our pride. Your perception of reality is just that — YOURS. It is not your husband's perception nor is it God's. God is the ONLY place you will find the total picture. He is the ultimate source of truth. He knows your thoughts better than you know them. He also has complete knowledge of your past, present, and future. He knows the spiritual warfare that has been at work in your family line for generations. He knows the results of every choice made by you and for you. He knows the same about your husband.

When my parents divorced, I recognized that I had learned many relationship skills that did not work. I didn't know what they were. I just knew that I had witnessed 19 years of their marriage, and what they had done did not work. You may be reflecting on your family now and wondering if you have the skills to make your marriage work. It is a good question to ask God. He is our wonderful counselor. He can use anything Satan meant for harm and redeem it for something much more wonderful than any of us could imagine (Genesis 50:20).

Nothing is too hard for God. As we recognize a relationship problem with our spouse, we can boast to God about it as our weakness. Second Corinthians 12:9–10 promises that God is sufficient to fill in the gaps of our imperfections. We can present to Him our weaknesses, and He will bring His power to rest on us. God is not waiting in heaven for you and your husband to get this right. He is waiting for both of you to admit that it is hard and you need His help.

You can invite God to reveal to both of you what is causing or could cause distance, resentment, or bitterness between you. Remember, He is generous with wisdom. He desires for you to see your sin — anything that separates you from Him and all that He has to give you. As you recognize your relationship challenges, you have a chance to see how amazing God is as healer. Every problem you have is a gift that when brought to Him, gives Him the opportunity to display His perfection.

In this spiritual battle, the enemy is waiting to tell you that this is too hard. He wants you to quit and will whisper that it is too risky to admit you don't have it all together. Fight him with the truth. Hold up your shield of faith in God who heals, who is patient, who sustains marriages, whose presence brings joy. Remind yourself that every trial is increasing your faith in God and that this particular issue is one more reason to rejoice (James 1:2–4).

The Bible is packed with true accounts of families with unhealthy boundaries and defense tactics. You and your husband are not going to deal with something that is new and worse. Solutions are found in applying God's love to yourselves and His Word to your life. You are going to grow and change into a greater likeness of Jesus. Stay in constant communication with God on these hard subjects. He is gentle. He is kind. He will lead you to wholeness. The gospel is good news and it is for you and your husband.

Prayer Prompt

Father, You created me and _____ for relationship with You. With great care, You have given me and

_____ Your own image so that in relationship we can experience Your love. Thank You for this gift of communion with You and each other. May Your light shine brightly in our marriage (Revelation 4:11; Genesis 1:27; Matthew 5:16).

You have loved the two of us faithfully, pouring out Your patience, kindness, gentleness, provisions, wisdom, and so much more. In Christ, _____ and I are blessed with all the spiritual blessings You have to offer. I believe that in Your perfect love for us, You have provided everything necessary for us to enjoy life together and in relationship with others (1 Corinthians 13:4–8; Matthew 7:11; James 1:5; Ephesians 1:3; John 10:10).

Because sin is a reality, both of us have experienced painful interactions with people who were and are significant to us. _____ and I are aware that emotional fallout from these events affect our marriage. This brings us to a greater awareness of our need for You and Your intervention. In faith, I give to you our burdens and heartaches, trusting that You are our healer (Romans 6:23; Philippians 4:19; Psalm 147:3; 1 Peter 5:7).

I celebrate the gift of freedom from sin and bondage that Jesus died to give both of us (Romans 8:2; Isaiah 61:1–3).

In Your love for us, please reveal the thoughts, feelings, attitudes, and beliefs that need to change. Let Your truths penetrate our minds and hearts. Your Word is alive and active. It is able to pierce the darkness and break off the lies we have believed and the unhealthy patterns that evolved. Help us to know the confidence, peace of mind, and freedom that comes from obeying You (Hebrews 4:12; Isaiah 32:17).

Let Your light and love dispel every falsehood presented to us as reality.

Let Your light and love dispel every falsehood presented to us as reality. Slay our fears, Lord. Demolish our pride.

Tear down the self-protective positions we have erected that do not serve us in this marriage (Psalm 139:23–24; 2 Corinthians 10:5).

Jesus, You modeled a life of forgiveness for us. Thank You for forgiving us before we ever recognized our sin and asked You to intervene. I choose for us a lifestyle of forgiveness in obedience to Your Word. Guide us, Holy Spirit, to live this out regardless of the cost. You are for us. We trust that forgiveness is something that will bring wholeness and healing. Let this be true for us, Lord (Luke 23:34; Matthew 6:12; Colossians 3:13).

I invite You to bring the healing that comes from forgiveness. Help us to forgive the following people for the pain we experienced:

1.

2.

3.

4

5.

6.

7.

Forgive us, Lord, for the ways we have hurt each other because of the unhealthy boundaries. You are the overcomer. Through You, Christ Jesus, we are more than conquerors. Let our minds be transformed by the power of Your Word (1 Corinthians 15:57; Romans 8:27, 12:2).

Teach us Your truth. Remodel our minds so that we have healthy boundaries in all of our relationships. We want to walk in Your light. Grant us the gift of mentors, teachers, counselors, and other truth-speakers to walk with us on this journey (Isaiah 2:5; Psalm 25:5, 121:2).

With Your leadership, we will limit our exposure to unhealthy relationships. Guide us to do so in love and with humility (Proverbs 20:24; Psalm 1:1; Colossians 3:12).

You are in this marriage, Jesus. We celebrate that with Your presence comes freedom and great joy (2 Corinthians 3:17; Psalm 16:11).

In Jesus, I pray.

Amen

A Wife's Call to Action

"Marriage is not slavery. It is based on a love relationship deeply rooted in freedom. Each partner is free from the other and therefore free to love the other. Where there is control, or perception of control, there is not love. Love only exists where there is freedom."[20] — *Boundaries in Marriage*, Dr. Henry Cloud and Dr. John Townsend

Is there any part of that quote that bothers you?

Is there any part of that quote that makes you breathe a sigh of relief?

Talk to God about it and find a time to discuss the quote and your feelings with your husband.

Chapter 36

Ignite the Aroma of Blessing and Forgiveness

Are these verses familiar to you?

> But I say to you who hear, Love your enemies, do good to those who hate you, bless those who curse you, pray for those who abuse you (Luke 6:27–28).

> Be merciful, even as your Father is merciful. Judge not, and you will not be judged; condemn not, and you will not be condemned; forgive, and you will be forgiven; give, and it will be given to you. Good measure, pressed down, shaken together, running over, will be put into your lap. For with the measure you use it will be measured back to you (Luke 6:36–38).

A life of forgiveness and blessing sets a Christian apart from unbelievers. Loving this way is an important step in following Jesus. He employed these principles as He washed the feet of His closest friends (disciples) knowing they would fail Him miserably the next day, the most anguish-filled day of His life.

God bless the counselor who listened to me complain one too many times about a conflict. She taught me the command from

Jesus to love your enemies. I remember giving her this look, "Are you serious? That is in the Bible?" And I knew that I had to obey in order to find peace.

David and I had received mail from someone who appeared to want to hurt us. It felt like the last straw. I lay on the couch, weeping and wondering, "How could anyone be this mean?" Both of us were consumed with thoughts of retaliation. I got myself together and drove around town. There in the driver's seat I began the journey of blessing and forgiving an enemy. I said to God, "In obedience to You, I choose to forgive _____. And I choose for myself the healing that forgiveness brings. I want You to bless them financially. Give them favor with their children. Let their friends be many. I hope they have great fellowship together. Help them, Lord, to enjoy their life and all the blessings You have waiting for them."

I spent three days verbalizing my choice of forgiveness and blessing over this enemy who had threatened our peace. Then I realized I was free from the constant barrage of angry thoughts toward them. Many years have passed, and I am still free of wishing bad things for them. The negative emotions I once harbored toward them were killed at the root.

Amazing! Jesus came to set the captives free. The teaching of Luke chapter 6 set this captive free in that relationship. There are some people that I forgive and bless and then later realize that I am still very angry. Each time I have to make the choice to forgive again and to bless them in some way.

Satan wants your mind to be a battlefield. He would love to see your marriage become the battlefield, too. He wants to steal, kill, and destroy it. He would like for you to see your husband as your enemy. Remember, God unites, and Satan causes division. You will not be wrestling against flesh and blood, but against the evil forces that are competing with God.

Decide today that you will protect your mind and marriage by offering forgiveness to your husband. This is your best defense in times of trouble. Work through the conflict, speak truth in love, seek counseling if the situation calls for it. But imitate Christ in forgiving him.

You and your husband may one day find yourself the target of someone's cruelty. Choosing to forgive and bless your enemy together will strengthen your marriage. In his book *The Three Battlegrounds*, Francis Frangipane explains:

> The battle you are in will soon become a meal to you, an experience that will nourish and build you up spiritually.[21]

Jesus explained that the portion we give is the portion we will get. "Give and it will be given to you." Whether you are giving forgiveness or the cold shoulder, you can expect to receive the same. The words found right after the Lord's Prayer are sobering.

> For if you forgive others their trespasses, your heavenly Father will also forgive you, but if you do not forgive others their trespasses, neither will your Father forgive your trespasses (Matthew 6:14–15).

If you are honest with yourself, you know you need forgiveness and mercy as much as the next new bride. Your pride wants to believe you are not nearly as wrong as your husband. But Jesus knew you were both going to fail, and He offers each of you new mercy every morning. Do yourself a favor and ask God to remind you of the relationships where you need to offer forgiveness and blessing. Take that first heavy step of obedience and offer these two gifts. Stay angry and bitter at the risk of destroying your own peace of mind and maybe your marriage.

Keep your eyes on Jesus, your perfect example for forgiving and blessing.

Prayer Prompt

I praise You, God, for Your gift of forgiveness to _____ and me. Your mercy covers our failures. Thank You for never giving up on either of us while we wrestle with selfishness and pride (Psalm 103:11–12, 145:8; Hebrews 13:5).

You are far more experienced with enemies than I am, Lord. Still You grant pardon after pardon because Your love is perfect. You give. You sacrifice. You amaze me (Micah 7:18; 1 John 4:18; Psalm 18:30, 145:9; 1 Corinthians 3:6; Hebrews 10:14).

Let this call to forgiveness and blessing change me at my very core so I can love even in difficult relationships. Shine a spotlight on my cruel thoughts. I want to repent and replace those thoughts with Your truth. Let Your thoughts about my enemies become my thoughts (Luke 6:26–38; Psalm 139:23).

Holy Spirit, compel me to forgive all who have caused me pain. I want to experience the healing that forgiveness brings. I want to trust Your leadership and reject the self-glorifying desire to vindicate myself (Matthew 6:15; Proverbs 3:3; Psalm 17:2; Isaiah 42:8).

Help me to recognize fear, worry, doubt, and self-pity as weapons in Satan's arsenal. I want to recognize them and protect myself with my shield of faith in You. Guide my husband in the same way so that we can share the mind of Christ (Ephesians 6:16; 1 Corinthians 2:16).

You have blessed us with more than our minds can imagine. Use _____ and me to be a reflection of You and a blessing to others (Ephesians 1:3, 3:20; 2 Corinthians 3:18).

Hear my prayer, Lord.

Amen

A Wife's Call to Action

Do you have an enemy today? Someone who occupies too much real estate in your mind? Someone who causes you to lose your cool and any indication that Christ might live in you? I want you

to practice blessing and forgiving them right now. Kick your obedience up a notch and bless your enemy. I know, I know. This is unlike
any battle scene you've ever imagined.

Really, the sky is the limit.

A blessing for your enemy can include but is not limited to

- praying for them
- sending a card or a gift
- saying something nice to them or about them to someone else
- really, the sky is the limit

You can choose to let them know you are doing something nice for
them. Or you can remain anonymous like a friend of mine who sent
his enemy a bouquet of flowers without signing the card.

Chapter 37

Recognize Emotional Reactions and Seek Healing

Marriage has a way of causing unresolved emotional issues to float to the surface. I did not know what to do with my emotions and reactions in my marriage to Michael.

Until I participated in biblical counseling on my own, I didn't begin to find freedom from my emotional pain. This happened during my marriage to David and it is the reason I am a much more joy-filled wife.

Are your reactions revealing that you brought a wounded heart to your marriage? What about your husband's reactions?

Here is a short list of emotional reactions that could reveal an underlying emotional wound that is in need of healing:

- anxiety, which often reveals itself through physical reactions

- uncontrolled anger, hostility, jealousy, antagonism, revenge

- inability to express anger, pretending everything is okay, martyrdom

- depression, powerlessness, pessimism, self-deprecation, dissatisfaction, despair

- confusion, indecision, dishonesty, distraction, distrust

- indifference, apathy, lack of emotion, preoccupation, disinterest, insensitivity, weariness

- humiliated, distant, secretive, victimized, offended, smothered, injured

- judgmental, ranting, scolding, disgusted, combative, pushy, neglectful

Emotional pain is real, it's heavy, and it can lead to really hard days in marriage. But it can be overcome. There is hope, and I'm living proof of that. Please do not let anyone lead you to believe that things will just "always be this way." Healing is Jesus' occupation. All throughout the gospels, Jesus healed. In the last decade, He has been healing me of self-hatred, perfectionism, and bitterness, which caused reactions like many of those listed above. He continues to reveal to me areas that need His healing touch.

As Christians, you and I have inherited all the spiritual blessings because Christ Jesus made us heirs (Ephesians 1:3–11). We can spend the rest of our days exploring the blessings of inheritance, which certainly includes emotional health!

We are dead to sin and alive in Christ. So we do not have to live in sin nor do we have to live reacting to the sin that hurt us. It does not have the right to rule our thoughts or behavior.

Do you believe that?

You chose life with Jesus, the living Word of God. Because Jesus lives in you, His power is within you. It is available to break the strongholds (areas where sin holds you captive) left by fear, abandonment, abuse, neglect, and more.

You can choose to reject fear and shame. God has not given you a spirit of fear. God's enemy serves fear to you. You have the right to reject it as freely as you would reject food that you did not order at a restaurant.

Power, love, and a sound, disciplined mind: these are three gifts God gives to you. Have you chosen them? You can choose to interact with these gifts daily. They are not for display on the shelf of your life. Regardless of your circumstances, you can employ Jesus' love, His power, and the soundness of His mind.

You may feel weak. But Jesus is not weak at all and He lives in you. The Bible says that you can choose to boast to Jesus that you have a weakness, and expect His power to rest on your life to overcome it or fill in the gap for you (2 Corinthians 12:9).

We can only love because God loved us first. You and your husband can choose to receive His love, to trust that He is loving. We all need Him to show us His extravagant love (Ephesians 3:19) — the love that Satan has worked diligently to hide.

Has God's extravagant love been obvious or hidden in your life? What about in your husband's life?

You can freely tell God that you do not feel love or feel loved. You can confess to Him that you are angry, lonely, and sometimes bitter and jealous. He will not be surprised and it will not disappoint Him. Pouring out your heart to Him is the safest thing you can do with your emotions. The great I AM will not react the way the people in your life have reacted to your heart and your hurt.

While you are wounded and waiting on your heart to be healed, you can rely on God to love your spouse through You. Emmanuel, God with you, is able to release love, kindness, patience, and gentleness through you. Invite Him to do it.

He is love, and He can use your mind, mouth, and body to deliver His love to your husband.

Your mind belongs to God. It's His design, and you surrendered it to Him when you said "Yes" to Jesus. It is His property to remodel and repurpose. On your own, you may not guard it well. You risk allowing elements of sinful behavior to open the door to destruction. But each time you choose to learn from the Bible and ask Jesus for His help, your mind will be renewed.

We are all restoration projects in progress. We do not possess every healthy thought and relationship skill. So we simply choose to invite Jesus' power to rest on our weaknesses. The wealth of heaven is at His disposal, and so He can work mightily to heal our thoughts and cause them to agree with His. All we have to do is continue to show up and have confidence in Him as our teacher and counselor. And while we are learning and agreeing with Him, He is intimately involved in our relationships. His patience, kindness, gentleness, and faithfulness are enough for what is needed today and tomorrow.

Jesus is enough!

Prayer Prompt

Amazing God, You sent Jesus to rescue me from myself. Thank You for pursuing me in my brokenness. I choose to open the eyes of my heart to see Your love for me (Isaiah 43:1–2).

I confess to You that I am weak, but I know that You are strong. I invite your power to rest on my weaknesses, particularly in the areas of _____, _____, _____, and _____ (2 Corinthians 12:9–10).

Jehovah Rapha, I am drawing near to You today for emotional healing. I want to experience the joy of freedom from the woundedness I feel. I trust You to hold our marriage together and strengthen it as You restore my mind to wholeness. I believe You sent Jesus and Your Word to heal me. So I will feast on Your Word, day and night. Your Word will satisfy my soul, and my lips will praise You. I will focus all of my being on following Your instructions, no matter how hard. My righteous living will be the forerunner to the peace and confidence You have promised (Psalm 63:5, 107:20; Isaiah 32:17).

Thank You for the gifts of Your love, power, and sound mind. I want to choose them and use them. Be my guide, Lord. Remind me that I am equipped with all that is needed to live in the freedom You died to give me. With Your power at work within me, I will train my mind to stay on You and things that are honorable, admirable, excellent, and pure (2 Timothy 1:7; Romans 8:2; Isaiah 26:3; Philippians 4:8).

I want all of these things for my husband as well, Lord. I draw near to You on his behalf, trusting You to draw near to him with Your love, power, and sound mind (James 4:8; 2 Timothy 1:7).

My mind and emotions are covered by the blood of Jesus (1 John 4:7).

In the name of Jesus, I pray.

Amen

A Wife's Call to Action

From the list of emotional reactions, record those that you see in yourself. Confess them to God and to your husband. Invite your husband to pray with you for healing in those areas.

Invite your husband to review the list and identify his own reactions. Pray with him, asking God for the healing he needs in those areas.

Chapter 38

Weave Your Histories into a New Tapestry

You married a unique masterpiece. He is God's unrepeatable miracle of a man. He is an individual that has been influenced by more words, actions, traditions, and expectations than either of you can name. Because you are an equally unique masterpiece, you have also been shaped by your relationships and experiences. Now, the two of you are one and somehow your histories must weave together to make a unique and whole life together.

As I write this book, David and I have been married for 16 years. That is over 5,800 days of blending his family, traditions, and past with mine. We can be so sure of each other one day, and the next day a new revelation has me shaking my head, amazed at what I did not know before this moment.

Becoming one takes time, patience, and faith that God is at work weaving the details of your uniqueness with your husband's. Impatience and the very common desire to have it all together will lead to discontentment. The fairy-tale ideal marriage we tend to exalt in our minds wants to be fulfilled quickly. We tend to focus on the ideal end result without considering the adventure of getting there.

Here is a quick glimpse of several threads that required time to become intertwined in my marriage to David.

We have opposite personalities. He's a very disciplined guy, a logical thinker, and a strategic, long-range planner. I am a global thinker, very spontaneous, sentimental, and easily distracted (or as I like to say, "interested in new things"). I had heard that opposites attract, but I lacked the knowledge of what to do with those differences in the day-to-day living.

We entered marriage having been influenced by unique parents and their own experiences. And we brought the scars from our first marriages to the table as well. We had different rules and traditions about birthdays, Christmas, and anniversaries.

David's children became my stepchildren. I was thrilled at the opportunity to be a stepmother. I do not have biological children and this was my chance at a family. Blending a family is challenging. So many people and their own histories influence the process.

David's family handled finances much differently than my family of origin. Our individual values were firmly ingrained in our spending. The differences were not resolved in one conversation, but have ebbed and flowed as we continue to become "us."

Because of my dad's personality and previous authority in my life, it was difficult to accept things about David that were very different than my dad. It is natural to compare, but it was not at all fair to the unique man I married. Dying to my expectations took time.

We both had our own "rules" about communication based on what we saw in our parents. Of course, we both thought our way was right because it was right to us. God has revealed the differences and the unhealthy aspects of what we've learned. But this occurred only as we have been faithful to ask Him for help.

Fear, pride, shame, and many more spiritual and emotional issues were hidden beneath the surface in each of us. Both of us reacted (still react in some instances) based on these unhealthy, unhealed areas. Sixteen years into the marriage, God is still revealing His power to heal us. It has been an adventure, a process that has required enduring love from each of us.

Have you detected tension arising as you face the differences in your experiences and your husband's?

Picture the act of weaving a cloth or a basket. It is not a "snap your fingers and it's done" process. The work is tedious and time consuming. Every strand is handled over and over again as it is blended with the other strands to make a whole.

Can you see the woven garment of your oneness with _____ displaying God's mysterious and creative power? Can you see the woven garment of oneness covering an area of God's kingdom with His light and love?

You will likely experience frustration and impatience in the bending needed to blend your lives together. It takes years to become a mature Christian who is able to consistently live out the truths: "It's not about me" and "I'm an important part of this union." Marriage, the weaving of two life stories into one, is a process that will not be rushed. God is patient with you as you allow Him to replace your will with His. Jesus has gone before you and me to prove that the self-denial required to love another deeply is humanly possible.

You and your husband's journey of being woven together will be somewhat similar to others. Yet it will most certainly be unique, because God has no need to create duplications of people or marriages. The similarities in our marriage tapestry and yours lie in this reality: God's perfect love and the devil's schemes are both present.

Decide today to surrender to the process. Trust God to shepherd your heart as you and your husband are woven into one sacred union.

Prayer Prompt

With my whole heart, Lord, I want to surrender to this process of weaving our stories into one. You are the awesome

Creator of our lives and now our one-flesh marriage. With great love for us, you have purposed us to complement each other. You have sewn into us very specific gifts and experiences to add to the joy of living with each other (Psalm 139:15; Mark 10:8).

You have perfect knowledge of the challenges we face. We can only imagine the issues that lie behind the scenes of our histories. You also know every sin-laden scheme the enemy has successfully used on us and the generations before us. But You are the God who restores and makes all things new (Romans 11:33; 1 Corinthians 1:25; Deuteronomy 30:3; 2 Corinthians 5:17).

You are the supernatural power needed to overcome our resistance to change and compromise. Please forgive us both for ways we have critically communicated to each other that our way is the right way. Let Your truth humble us. You are the potter. We are the clay. Help us to see our own need for You as much as we see each other's need (Matthew 19:26; 1 Corinthians 15:57; James 4:10; Isaiah 64:8).

You have perfect wisdom. But we too often rely on the world's wisdom and ourselves. Transform us into a husband and wife team desiring to follow Your lead. Your Word is the perfect source of light for our path (Proverbs 3:5–7; Romans 12:2; Psalm 119:105).

Grant us the patience and faithfulness we need to weather the hard days. Load our hearts with the extra portions of mercy we need for ourselves and for each other (Galatians 5:22; Psalm 23:6).

Let every facet of our sacred union be used by You to bring honor and glory to Your name (Ephesians 2:10; 1 Corinthians 10:31).

In Jesus' name, we pray.

Amen

A Wife's Call to Action

List three things about your life experiences or family traditions that seem to clash with your husband's.

Ask God for the faith of a mustard seed or greater to believe He can use those differences to strengthen and grow your marriage.

Think of an upcoming event or situation where one of these differences will be highlighted (Christmas, birthday, bill paying, vacation planning, etc.). Invite your husband to a discussion about it and to pray with you about it.

Chapter 39

Praying the Names of God for Your Marriage

Throughout the Bible we see God identified by many defining names or titles. This is God's way of communicating to us His role in our life. Jesus and the Holy Spirit are also given names to help us know who they are.

When you work for a company or a ministry, one of your first tasks is to learn the departments that handle the various types of work within the company. Maybe you use a directory or an organizational chart to find the person you need to communicate with about your project. You do not need to waste time talking to someone in shipping about a human resources issue.

Knowing God's roles in your life and in your marriage helps you to know what He can do, so you are confident that you can trust Him with your current need. When we know that He is our shepherd, we can ask Him to lead us in big and small decisions and keep us safe. We do not have to waste time looking to someone else to be our guide.

This chapter does not cover every name of God nor the names of Jesus or the Holy Spirit. You will find a broad overview of God's roles in your life. Each name is listed with Scripture references and a one-sentence prayer prompt to help you start praying the names of God or communicating with Him about His roles in your life.

Jehovah Jireh: The Lord is my Provider

Genesis 22:14

Jehovah Jireh, help me and _____ to experience You as the provider in our marriage.

Jehovah Nissi: The Lord is my Banner

Exodus 17:15

Jehovah Nissi, You are victorious and I want to live out our marriage under Your victory banner.

Jehovah Shalom: The Lord is my Peace

Judges 6:24

Jehovah Shalom, _____ and I invite You to be the source of our peace and rest in our marriage.

Jehovah Sabbaoth: The Lord of Hosts

1 Samuel 1:3, 17:45

Jehovah Sabbaoth, I want our marriage to be under Your leadership, Your command.

Jehovah Maccaddeshcem: The Lord our Sanctifier

Exodus 31:13

Jehovah Maccaddeshcem, purify our hearts so that we live pure lives, different from the ways of the world.

Jehovah Rapha: God is my Healer

Exodus 15:26

Jehovah Rapha, we celebrate that You have the power to heal everything: mind, body, and soul.

Jehovah Ro'i: The Lord my Shepherd

Psalm 23:1

Jehovah Ro'i, we choose You as our shepherd so that we remain safe from evil in Your constant care.

Jehovah Shammah: The Lord is there

Ezekiel 48:35

Jehovah Shammah, our hearts and our home are blessed because You reside there.

Jehovah Tsidkenu: The Lord our Righteousness

Jeremiah 23:6

Jehovah Tsidkenu, You have washed our sins with the Blood of Jesus, making us right with You and giving us permission to be in Your presence.

El Shaddai: God Almighty

Genesis 17:1, 28:3, 35:11; Exodus 6:1; Psalm 91:1–2

El Shaddai, I rely on You as the mightiest One who is able to help us, save us, and thwart the evil strategies of the enemy.

El Elyon: The Most High God

Genesis 14:19; Psalm 9:2; Daniel 7:18, 22, 25

El Elyon, there is no one in higher authority than You, so I dedicate my life and our marriage to serving You.

El Olam: The Everlasting God

Genesis 16:13

El Olam, I am determined to walk in obedience to You, my never-ending, never-changing authority.

Adonai: Master, Owner

Genesis 18:2, 40:1; 1 Samuel 1:15; Exodus 21:1–6; Joshua 5:14

Adonai, convict me and _____ when we begin to see ourselves and others in charge of our lives and decisions.

Father

Matthew 7:11; James 1:17; Hebrews 12:5–11; John 15:16, 16:23; Ephesians 2:18, 3:15; 1 Thessalonians 3:11

Father, help us to see You as our Father and to relate to the role of father from the standpoint of Your character instead of a human man.

*Jehovah and Yahweh are often used interchangeably. Use whichever you are more comfortable with.

A Wife's Call to Action

Did you learn something new about God's role in your marriage in this chapter? Which one surprised you? Did one of them help you breathe a sigh of relief?

Pick one of those and spend ten minutes researching the Bible reference(s) associated with that name. Search the Internet for biblical commentary on that name of God. I use Biblehub.com and scroll down the page for several commentaries.

How would your life change if you relied on God to perform that role in your life and marriage?

Chapter 40

One-Sentence Prayers

There are days and seasons in your marriage when you will need to hang on to one single truth from God's Word. This chapter offers simple, one-sentence prayers based on the main topics covered in this book.

You and your husband can use this section throughout your marriage to find one that fits what you are facing. But I want to encourage you to let these prayers lead you to a life of praying the words of God back to Him. Train your mind to read the Bible, looking for truths that are waiting to be prayed and lived out in your beautiful marriage.

Confidence in God

With You as my Lord, I will have nothing to fear (Psalm 23:1).

Help me to feel safe in Your presence because You are where my help comes from (Psalm 91).

Thank You for the ability to protect my husband and me from the enemy (2 Thessalonians 3:3).

Thank You for arming me with all that is needed to be victorious in life and in my marriage (Ephesians 6:11–18; Psalm 62:7).

Thank You for supplying all our needs and making that supply available through our relationship with Jesus (Philippians 4:19).

I praise You for Your incredible love that protects me (Psalm 4:8).

Thank you for loving me and _____ perfectly, completely, and eternally (1 John 4:8; 1 Corinthians 13:13).

Thank You for the gift of Your power, love, and sound mind (2 Timothy 1:7).

Your Word is my defense against Satan's lies and schemes that are set to destroy me and my marriage (John 8:32).

I commit to standing under Your leadership and following Your commands (1 John 5:3).

Thank You, Jesus, for praying for me according to God's desire for my life (Romans 8:27, 34).

Dependence on God

God, I am completely relying on You for help to stand up to the hard days in my marriage (Colossians 1:11).

Help me to grasp the reality of your love for me and for _____ (Ephesians 3:14–19).

Fuel within me a never-ending passion to know and live by Your Word and truth (Psalm 119:20).

Work in me an unshakeable faith that You are the source of my help to love _____ the way he needs to be loved by me (Mark 9:23; Hebrews 12:2–3).

Let Your power and love for me and _____ guide us away from temptation, bitterness, and other schemes of the enemy (2 Timothy 1:7; Matthew 6:13; Ephesians 4:31).

Renew us by the power of Your Word so that we are not vulnerable to the enemy's attacks (Romans 12:2; Ephesians 6:11–12).

Replace any words and images that could destroy the good thing _____ and I said "Yes" to with Your truth (Ephesians 4:22–24).

With Your help, I can avoid the lies, distractions, and schemes Satan has planned (John 14:26).

I want to enjoy the healing and the peace that knowing You brings (Isaiah 26:3).

I want to spend the rest of our marriage relying on You (Proverbs 3:5).

Guide me away from trusting myself and the many options presented to me by the world (Proverbs 3:5).

Teach me, Lord, to incorporate this armor You have provided into my every thought, feeling, word, and action (Ephesians 6:11–18; Psalm 19:14).

We need You as our guide, our hiding place, our fortress, our faithful protector (Psalm 18:2).

I want to pray about everything and rely on You always, regardless of the internal and spiritual resistance I feel (Colossians 1:11; Jeremiah 33:3).

Work in me a desire to know You more than I want fame, wealth, and anything else the enemy uses to distract me (Matthew 16:24–25).

I need Your help to guard my heart against bitterness, selfishness, and temptation to pursue the attention of other men and other things this world offers (Proverbs 4:23, 23:26).

Help me cling to specific verses in Your Word that will help me to experience Your love for me, my husband, and others (Proverbs 4:13).

Engrave Your Word on my mind and heart and let it transform me into a sweet aroma to You and to _____ (2 Corinthians 2:14–15).

Convict me daily so that I can repent and strengthen my commitment to You and _____ (John 16:8).

I rely on Your victorious power over sin to help us keep our marriage bed pure (Romans 6:14; Hebrews 13:4).

Open my eyes to Your wisdom on how to be the wife of _____ (James 1:5).

Thinking God's Way about Myself

I choose to agree with Your thoughts about me and to be the woman and wife You designed me to be (Jeremiah 29:11).

Let the power of Your truth overcome Satan's lies about who You are and who I am to You (John 8:32).

Break down the walls of fear and pride that keep me from knowing who I became when I embraced Jesus' sacrificial love on the Cross (Proverbs 16:18, 29:25).

I choose to put on the truth of who I am according to Your Word (Isaiah 61:10).

Thinking God's Way about My Husband

Give me wisdom to see _____ the way You see him (Isaiah 11:2).

Remind me of _____'s value to You and to me (Isaiah 43:4).

Teach me to honor _____ with my thoughts, my words, and my actions (Ephesians 5:33).

Help me to resist the temptation to focus on _____'s weaknesses or imperfections (Galatians 5:16; Mark 14:38).

Inspire me with Your endless creativity to speak of _____ and to him in ways that agree with Your thoughts of him (2 Peter 1:21).

Use me to bless _____ with declarations of Your truth (Jeremiah 1:9–12).

You see your son _____, rejoice and say, he is very good, and I agree! (Genesis 1:31).

Thinking God's Way about Marriage:

Lead me, Lord Jesus, to think and act on Your thoughts about marriage (Deuteronomy 13:4; Colossians 2:3).

I will worship You, God, by submitting to Your Word and honoring Your plan for marriage (Psalm 119:1; Hebrews 13:4).

God, I surrender my preconceived plans for success in marriage, and salute You as my ultimate authority (Isaiah 46:10).

Reveal to _____ and me what we have committed to in our marriage (Ephesians 1:17, 5:21–33).

I want to honor You in my marriage by loving my husband faithfully, sacrificially, and joyfully (Romans 12:10).

Bring mature Christian couples into our lives to model submission, love, and intimacy as taught in Your perfect Word (Proverbs 27:17; Titus 2:3–5).

A Wife's Call to Action

Choose two of the following Scripture references and write your own one-sentence prayers based on the message in the verse.

Ephesians 3:16

James 4:7

1 John 4:1

Philippians 4:8

Colossians 1:9

Subscribe to **Marriage Armor for the #PrayingBride** to get one-sentence prayers based on Scripture delivered to your inbox daily or in a weekly digest. Go to prayersfornewbrides.com/marriage-armor to sign up.

Epilogue

Abuse in Marriage

You may find yourself in a marriage that feels unsafe. His actions and his words may leave you feeling small and unworthy of love. You are not alone. Unfortunately, some wives find their hearts, minds, and sometimes their bodies critically wounded by their husbands.

If you are being physically or emotionally abused, tell someone today. Satan does his best work in the dark corners of secrets.

Jesus, the light of the world, is able to overcome the power of darkness. Exposing the truth is your first and most important step to freedom and hopefully complete restoration of your marriage.

The prayers of God's people can bring breakthrough.

When you are in the throes of marriage stress, you must have prayer support. Your wounded heart may struggle to hope and to pursue God. You need to let others in and invite them to pray with you and for you and your family. People who regularly pursue God and hear from Him are the valiant warriors you need on the front line of this battle. Do not delay in finding them.

You may need to physically remove yourself from your spouse and your home. You may need to find a safe place to live. God employed physical boundaries to keep people safe. Remember how baby Moses was hidden in the water to keep him from being killed. God intervened for Moses, and He will do the same for you.

I plead with you to give God time to intervene in the heart of your husband. Fear will guide you to take matters into your own hands. Moses once took a crisis into his own hands instead of following God's instructions. Because of this, Moses never stepped foot into the Promised Land.

God did not give you a spirit of fear. He gave you love, power, and a sound mind. His wisdom for you will agree with each of those attributes. His love for you can sustain you while you wait for personal healing for yourself and your husband. His power in you can help you to confront the abuse and the abuser while remaining a person of peace. His sound, well-controlled mind will empower you to grow mentally strong in a situation that threatens to steal your self-control.

God can make a way where there is no other way for your husband and your marriage. But, ultimately, your husband has to respond to God's voice. There are tragic stories of that not happening. In those cases, I believe God will release you. He will give you wise counsel and wisdom that could only come from His heart to yours. Listen to Him, friend. Be led by Him.

If your marriage is dissolved, and you remain steadfast in God, there is so much hope. He is able to redeem your life. He promises to give you a double portion for the shame you have endured and cause you to rejoice in the inheritance He gives to you (Isaiah 61:7). His ways are beyond our understanding and His mercy is always bringing us more than we deserve.

God is able to do far more than all that we ask or think, according to the power at work within us (Ephesians 3:20).

Appendix

Reinforcements

Visit PrayersforNewBrides.com for Recommended Resources and These Free Downloads

Prayer for the Couple Written for Parents and In-laws
Prayer for the Couple Written for Wedding Party, Close Friends, & Mentors
Prayer for the Couple Written for Children from Previous Marriages
Covenant to Honor & Defend til Death Do Us Part

Books

Prayers that Avail Much. Volumes 1,2,3 by Germaine Copeland
Wife After God by Jennifer Smith
Sacred Influence by Gary Thomas
The DNA of Relationships by Gary Smalley
Love & Respect by Emerson Eggerichs
Anger to Intimacy by Gary Smalley & Ted Cunningham
4 Days to a Forever Marriage by Gary & Norma Smalley
The Screwtape Letters by C.S. Lewis
The Wall Around Your Heart by Mary DeMuth
The Meaning of Marriage by Timothy Keller
Live a Praying Life by Jennifer Kennedy Dean
Fun Loving You by Ted Cunningham
The Three Battlegrounds by Francis Frangipane
Believing God by Beth Moore

DVD Series

His Needs, Her Needs by Willard Harley Jr.

Ministries

National Institute for Marriage — nationalmarriage.com
Smalley Institute — smalley.cc
Authentic Intimacy — authenticintimacy.com

Blogs, Websites, & Online Communities

Ephesians 5:33 Wife — http://ephesianswife.blogspot.com
Million Praying Women — http://millionprayingwomen.com
Start Marriage Right — http://startmarriageright.com
Imperfect Wives — http://theimperfectwives.org/
Faith-Focused Wives Facebook Community, https://facebook.com/groups/faithfocusedwives/

Endnotes

1. Timothy Keller, *The Meaning of Marriage: Facing the Complexities of Commitment with the Wisdom of God* (New York: Dutton, 2011).

2. C.S. Lewis, *The Screwtape Letters* (New York: HarperCollins, 2009), p. 164, http://rightwingnews.com/uncategorized/rwns-favorite-quotes-from-the-screwtape-letters/.

3. Brennan Manning, *All is Grace: A Ragamuffin Memoir* (Peabody, MA: David C. Cook, 2011).

4. A.W. Tozer, *The Knowledge of the Holy* (New York: HarperCollins, 1978), p. 1.

5. From George Washington's first State of the Union address, January 8, 1790.

6. Jennifer Smith, *The Unveiled Wife* (Wheaton, IL: Tyndale Momentum, 2015).

7. E.M. Bounds, *Purpose in Prayer* (Chicago, IL: Moody Press, n.d.), p. 9–10.

8. http://www.happywivesclub.com/marriage-quotes/.

9. Taken from *Living Free in Christ* by Neil Anderson (Ventura, CA: Regal Books, 1993).

10. Francis Frangipane, *The Power of Covenant Prayer* (Lake Mary, FL: Charisma House, 1998), p. 5.

11. Beth Moore, *Believing God* (Nashville, TN: Broadman & Holman, 2004).

12. http://www.pearlofgreatvalue.com/prayerquotes_000.php.

13. Stormie Omartian, *The Power of a Praying Wife* (Eugene, OR: Harvest House, 1997).

14. Gary Thomas, *Sacred Marriage* (Grand Rapids, MI: Zondervan, 2000), p. 125.

15. Mark Batterson, *The Circle Maker: Praying Circles around Your Biggest Dreams and Greatest Fears* (Grand Rapids, MI: Zondervan, 2012), chapter 2.

16. Oswald Chambers, *My Utmost for His Highest* (1924).

17. William Law, *The Works of the Reverend William Law*, Volume 3 (privately printed for G. Moreton Publisher, 1893), p. 214, books. google.com/books?id=ZDoZAQAAIAAJ.

18. C.S. Lewis, *Mere Christianity*, http://www.cslewisinstitute.org/webfm_send/116.

19. Dr. Henry Cloud and Dr. John Townsend, *Boundaries: When to Say Yes and When to Say No to Take Control of Your Life* (Grand Rapids, MI: Zondervan Pub. House, 1992).

20. Dr. Henry Cloud and Dr. John Townsend, *Boundaries in Marriage* (Grand Rapids, MI: Zondervan Publishing House,1999).

21. Os Hillman, "Peace — A Weapon Against Satan," Marketplace Leaders, http://www.marketplaceleaders.org/peace-a-weapon-against-satan/.

MEET THE
AUTHOR

Jennifer O. White has a bachelor's degree in social work, with a minor in marketing, the spiritual gifts of mercy and shepherding, and a passion to help others know their worth despite their failings. She taught Sunday school classes, small groups, women's Bible studies in person and on-line, and currently teaches at JenniferOWhite.com about pursuing a relationship with God through prayer.

New Leaf Press

Connect with Jennifer online:

JENNIFEROWHITE.COM

FACEBOOK.COM/**JENNIFEROWHITE**

TWITTER.COM/**JENNIFEROWHITE**